Wood Projects for the Garden

Projects Editor:
R. J. De Cristoforo

Designed by
Craig Bergquist

Photography by
William Aplin
Michael Landis
Clyde Childress

Front cover photo by
Michael Landis

Contents

Wood in the garden

**It is almost impossible to talk about wood in the garden without getting philosophical.
We would like to share with you some of the thoughts, beliefs, and appealing fancies we heard as we compiled this book.**

Whenever you plant a shrub or tree, you are planting wood — brown, gray, black; young, greenish, and supple, or old, gnarled, and mossy; strong and massive, or delicate and lacy.

The idea in most plantings is, at least partially, to appeal to your own eyes. Spring growth, summer lushness, fall color, winter silhouettes—shadow, color, change, all year around.

The same goes for building with wood. You won't get growth or lushness, but you will get color, silhouettes, shade, and change all year around.

Wood is the present and the future

Trees, hedges, rambunctious vines, all protect from the sun, the wind, and when necessary, the outside world.
So do overheads, fences, screens, lattices.

Plant a big tree or hedge, or build an overhead or deck or picnic table, and you plant or build a future — an environment for the years ahead.

Every family that builds a garden lives with long-term visions. The immediate needs might be for tricycle runs and bicycle storage, billowing drying yards, swings and scrimmage fields and soft places to tumble down upon. The middle pleasures might be in efficient storage, convenient aids, expansive entertainment amenities. The later satisfactions might be a hammock strung between two anchoring spots that gets both sun and afternoon shade, an interesting plant to have breakfast with, a safe and comfortable tenting area to sleep visiting grandchildren, and fuel for fires on cold winter evenings.

Every family that builds a garden thinks about a place for action and conviviality, as well as a place for aloneness and contentment. They think of a place to feel at home in, a place to return to, a place to remember with fondness.

Wood is change

A lath overhead won't provide as many surprises as will a seedling from a one-gallon can growing from sapling to youth to maturity. But it will change your garden's shadow patterns and your living patterns far more quickly.

◁
The contrast between this piece of twisted driftwood and the surrounding stand of horsetails emphasizes the charms and characteristics of both.

A grapestake fence won't provide the seasonal gifts of a pyracantha hedge, but it will provide privacy much sooner.

A redwood deck won't produce the same green vista as a sweep of healthy lawn, but it will quickly turn a part of your garden into a usable "room."

All wood—lath, fences, decks, containers, whatever—will produce its own surprise, change, action. Wood mellows, it ages, it bleaches out, or deepens in color. The elements work on a man-made structure much as they

This weathered stump, used as a bird-feeding station, attracts as many birds as when it was a tree.

do on driftwood. They wash it, dry it, soak it, bake it—wearing away the soft spots and finding all the contours.

Wood companions well

It's a mistake to think of any garden structure strictly as a substitute for plants. You are never looking for a substitute only. You are looking for a companion for the plants you have, or plants that you would like to have.

What grape vine or wisteria or wandering rose isn't in search of a trellis to climb, an overhead to smother, a lattice to explore? What hollyhock or berry or delphinium or lantana wouldn't do better with a fence to bask against?

Take any spreading chestnut or oak or maple. Would it fondly nurture a feeding station for migratory birds? Would it stand all the prouder if it held a swing for the children? Would it hold its head even higher with importance if it had a neighborhood hideaway in its branches?

Wood is . . . well, face it, wood is immortal

It's almost as if wood had a collective memory. At home in the garden while it was green and growing and individual, it remains at home in the garden for a long and productive afterlife.

A redwood tree is a significant, scale-making, sky-scratching backdrop in any garden, if you happen to have a redwood tree. If you don't, it has contributions to make anyway. Redwood is handy and handsome as a garden floor, in rounds or boards, or decking; as furniture, as planters, as edging, or as small containers.

A bamboo grove can be a beautiful, thick, troublesome divider wall if it happens to separate you and your neighbor. If it doesn't, it's happy to serve humbly as an inexpensive fence, an inset in a gate, even a stake for a leggy tomato.

Wood works, and it works well, hard, and long. It works while it's growing, and it keeps right on working after it retires.

Consider a dead tree. Instead of chopping it down, leave it where it is and plant a fast-growing vine to clothe it.

In a few short months the skeleton will cease to be a skeleton—and, you will no longer be "The people down the block with a dead tree in their yard."

You will be the people with a high-reaching, wide-spreading, shade-producing overhead. It will be a strong structure that supports berries, fruits, flowers, leaves—even birds. And, in all probability, its share of caterpillars, red spider mites, and thrips.

Don't ever consider it merely as a dead tree. By topping it off waist-high, knee-high, or lower, and putting a chair next to it, you've "built" a table. Put a table next to it, and you've built a stool.

Of lop it off at chin, shoulder, or tiptoe-stretching height, and incorporate a bit of whimsey. Hollow out the top, and use it as a planter. Top it with a tray, and it's a bird's feeding station. Or attach pegs for the garden hose, a hanging basket or two, or wet beach towels.

Carve it into a sculpture. Maybe a tiki, with giant ferns and garden torches set out behind it.

Wood lasts . . . endures . . . serves

It likes the great outdoors, and seems to know that it belongs. It's used to living in human scale, and seems to know that it's appreciated. Moss, looking for a home, asks no questions as to whether the wood is still a tree or not.

'Wood in the garden' is such a friendly, familiar, everyday thought that, upon first approach, no one seemed to have

much to say about it. However, with a bit of probing, different images of what those words might mean surfaced.

Some people immediately think big—overheads, fences, decks. Others think small—containers, chopping boards, salad bowls, even the sweet-smelling woodiness of sawdust mulch.

Some people conjure up rather elaborate visions of man-made structures. Others only want to help nature design . . . by bringing out the grain of a tabletop, or incorporating driftwood into a mobile.

Some think primarily in terms of visual effects. Others consider other senses: wood's smell on a rainy day, the texture underfoot, the echo of footpads upon it.

Some think brand new, some think traditionally old. Many are very literal—'wood in the garden' is what grows in the garden: their woody trees and shrubs.

A 'woods in the garden'

A few wood-loving gardeners take it one step further — using wood to create woodsiness. They spread ground bark mulch beneath a rhododendron to move it back into the forest. They surround low-growing junipers with wood chips, and don't care if the junipers are slow to spread (they've achieved the woodsy effect they wanted).

Black plastic to stop the weeds, bark chunks to hide the plastic, and they have a weedless forest.

To them, wood is less a building material than it is food for millions of insects, molds, fungus, and micro-organisms. To them—as they toss a stick of wood onto the compost pile—wood is not something to keep, but something to feed into Nature's cycle.

Capturing its mystique

So what is there about wood? A landscape architect might answer: "Wood makes a strong statement. It lends itself to good design."

A nurseryman: "It fits in. It's practical. The eye is used to seeing it with plants."

A true gardener: "My plants like to live with wood. Behind, under, over, in front . . . silhouetted, enclosed, staged, pocketed . . . it doesn't matter. The plants like it, I like it."

A sensual, sensitive man: "It's soft. It smells good. It feels good. It doesn't clatter."

A purist: "It's inobtrusive. Nature-colored. It doesn't clutter."

A homemaker: "It's homey. It belongs. I'm homey. So do I."

A homemaker who does the cleaning up: "Just hose it down. It's wonderful."

A child: "It feels good, barefooted."

A designer: "It takes to anything. It forms modules. Shave it, bend it, crush it . . ."

A traditionalist: "It was good enough for grandpa."

We can't in this one book, cover in depth all of the viewpoints of all of the wood-loving, garden-loving people of the world. But, we can begin to round up, illustrate, admire, and pass on building instructions for some of the specific woody satisfactions that a few dozen people have shared with us.

For the most part, we limit ourselves here to things that are small in scale—projects that might require as little as an hour, at the most a couple of hardworking weekends.

The rough-sawn texture of a wood slab provides a pleasing, contrasting background for this luxuriant succulent.

All you will need to build a simple box.

Project boxes

Here and on the next 15 pages, consider the various kinds of wooden boxes made to hold soil in which plants are grown.

For the moment, forget pots, although there's a place in our garden for pots of every size. Boxes of wood can be wider, longer, or taller than any pot we have seen. And, most importantly, we can *build* a box.

As gardens grow smaller; as patio floors, decks, and balconies become the gardening space, we learn to garden in boxes.

Simple box

Given a reasonably sharp hand saw, a hammer, a square, and some nails, you are equipped to build a square or rectangular box. To illustrate the simple procedure we have shown the assembly of a box 12 inches wide, 16 inches long, and 6 inches deep.

Skills necessary: 1. Make square cuts with the saw. 2. Hammer nails flush with the wood without leaving hammer marks.

We used a 3-piece wood bottom but plywood bottom in drawing is easier to assemble.

Of course no planter box is finished without drainage holes. So add a brace and bit or an electric drill to the basic tools. Bore ¼- or ½-inch holes about 4 to 6 inches apart. Cover holes with screening material such as aluminum or fiberglass fly screen to prevent soil from washing through.

◊

Drain holes are essential to a planter box. A power drill or hand drill will do the job equally well.

The simple box takes on a new look with a simple planting.

Simple, but elegant in its own way.

Step by step to a simple box

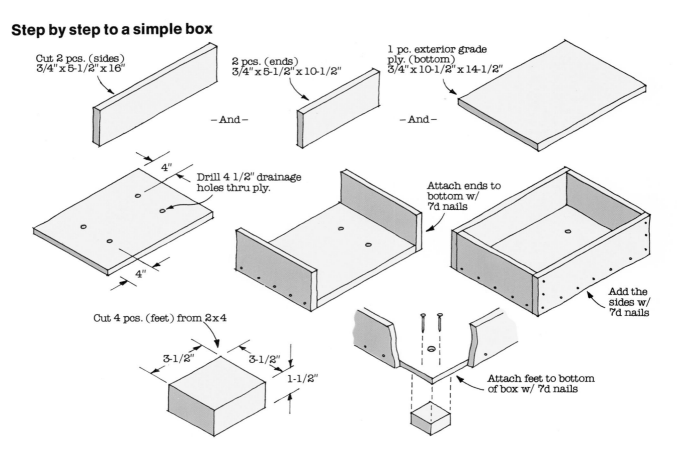

Cut 2 pcs. (sides)
3/4" x 5-1/2" x 16"

2 pcs. (ends)
3/4" x 5-1/2" x 10-1/2"

—And—

1 pc. exterior grade
ply. (bottom)
3/4" x 10-1/2" x 14-1/2"

—And—

4"

Drill 4 1/2" drainage
holes thru ply.

4"

Attach ends to
bottom w/
7d nails

Add the
sides w/
7d nails

Cut 4 pcs. (feet) from 2 x 4

3-1/2"   3-1/2"   1-1/2"

Attach feet to bottom
of box w/ 7d nails

Various modular displays can be arranged by using the wooden sleeves and reversible bases of the multipurpose box.

Single box with 6-inch pots of begonias resting on reversible base.

Multipurpose box

If you bring home a dozen 'Petite' marigolds, the 3-inch-deep box will show off the 8-inch-high plants better than a deep box.

But, if the marigolds are the variety 'Hawaii,' better use the 6-inch-deep box.

This box starts with a 6-inch depth and varies in height in multiples of 2 and 4 inches. Your box might be any combination of depths.

More combinations are possible when you have the components for two complete boxes.

Above left: *We used 6- and 7-inch pots in this box display.* Right: *Same boxes are used full depth to house a tomato in a 5-gallon can.*

Our multipurpose box is dimensioned to suit the container and pot sizes shown at the right. The project consists of an invertible base, plus two sleeves which slip over the projecting corner posts. Either sleeve may be used regardless of the base position. For example, use the base bottom-down and with the large sleeve, for a 5-gallon can, or with the bottom up and the small sleeve, for low pots.

Attach the ends of the base to the corner posts and then add the sides. Size the bottom to fit and then cut the notches for the corner posts.

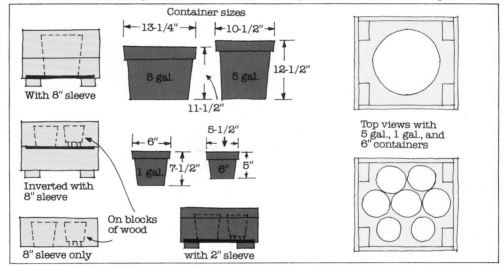

Container sizes

With 8" sleeve

13-1/4"   10-1/2"

5 gal.   5 gal.   12-1/2"

11-1/2"

Inverted with 8" sleeve

6"   5-1/2"

1 gal.   7-1/2"   6"   5"

On blocks of wood

8" sleeve only

with 2" sleeve

Top views with 5 gal., 1 gal., and 6" containers

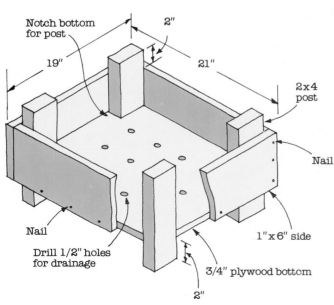

Notch bottom for post

2"

19"   21"

2x4 post

Nail

Nail

Drill 1/2" holes for drainage

3/4" plywood bottom

2"

1"x6" side

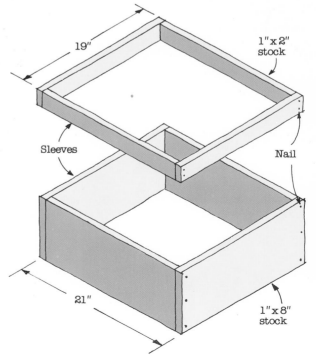

19"

1"x2" stock

Sleeves

Nail

21"

1"x8" stock

Boxes "planted" with cans in 15-gallon, 5-gallon, and 1-gallon sizes. Slide the can gently into the box . . .

Closed container top can be used as a table.

Hide-a-can boxes

Many large plants from the nursery will grow for months or years in the containers they come in. If you are not content to look at the nursery container, but don't want to transplant it immediately, we suggest the hide-a-can box.

Made of lath, it is economical and surprisingly good looking. The cover of the box allows the plant container to serve as a low table—a convenient resting place for empty glasses.

. . . Two part cover conceals it from view.

A variation on the box idea using a movable front panel to hide the cans. For results see photo page 29.

Study the drawing and the chart carefully before you cut material for the hide-a-can box. The best procedure is to assemble the sides of the box (lath pieces to body cleats) as separate units and then put them together by driving the 8d nails at each corner. Attach the end lath pieces last, since they may require trimming to fit.

Assemble the lid after the body is finished so you can check its overall size directly on the box. The center opening may be square or round. If square, cut two or three of the middle pieces shorter than the others before nailing to the lid cleats. It's better to cut a round opening after assembly. In either case, saw the lid in half as the last step.

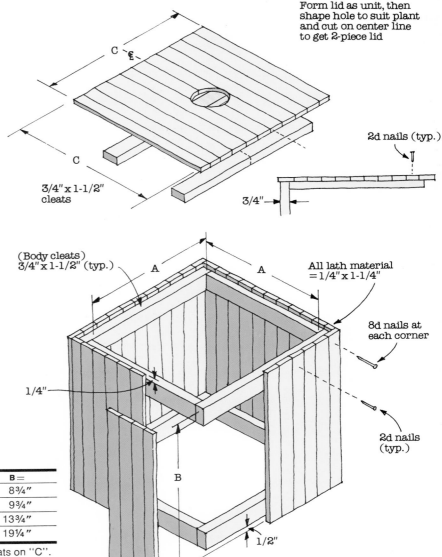

Form lid as unit, then shape hole to suit plant and cut on center line to get 2-piece lid

C

3/4" x 1-1/2" cleats

2d nails (typ.)

3/4"

(Body cleats) 3/4" x 1-1/2" (typ.)

A   A

All lath material = 1/4" x 1-1/4"

8d nails at each corner

1/4"

B

2d nails (typ.)

1/2"

How to determine dimensions

Size of Can	A =	B =
1-gallon	7"	8¾"
2-gallon	9"	9¾"
5-gallon	12"	13¾"
15-gallon	15½"	19¼"

Dimension ''B'' includes ¾" for the lid cleats on ''C''.
In all cases, ''C'' = ''A'' plus 1½"

Assorted vegetable boxes in our garden.

Vegetable boxes— various depths

When growing vegetables in boxes the depth of the box is the critical measurement. After three years of growing vegetables in containers we settled on the collection of sizes shown on these pages.

In our trials we have kept in mind portability, as well as frequency of watering and fertilizing. The shallower the box, the less weight but the more frequent is the water and fertilizing. Here are our ideas of minimum depths:

4 inches deep—lettuce, turnips, radishes, beets, and all the low-growing herbs.

6 inches deep—chard, kohlrabi, short carrots such as 'Baby Finger,' and the root crops listed above.

8 inches deep—bush beans, cabbage, eggplant, peppers, bush cucumbers.

10 inches deep—cauliflower, broccoli, Brussels sprouts.

12 inches deep—parsnips, salsify, long-rooted carrots, tomatoes.

Carrot box (above) and beet box (below).

Gayfeather (Liatris)

Black bamboo (Phyllostachys nigra)

Let the box fit the plant

We took this old truism seriously and shopped our favorite nursery with boxes in mind. The results of our shopping and box building are shown on these pages. Whether or not we let the box fit the plant is for you to decide. You probably have your own ideas about what is fitting.

Right: Ternstroemia gymnanthera
Below: Pieris 'Variegata' *with Scotch moss.*

Artichoke

'Ruby Ball' cabbage and 'Bibb' Lettuce

Japanese Black Pine (Pinus thunbergii)

Study of supports

The box may sit on the ground, on brick, or concrete paving. In any situation it will look better and serve you longer if it has legs or is blocked up above ground. Let there be air space beneath the bottom of the box.

As the photos on these pages show, the plant and the box often are enhanced by being elevated. A stump, or a section of railroad tie or telephone pole can often give a plant or box the stature it deserves.

Woodworker's boxes

To the wood enthusiast, odds and ends of 2 x 4's, or any dimension, are an inviting challenge. "What can I make out of that scrap?"

Let the box match the plant. Let the box match your woodworking skills and the tools at hand.

When the box is to be viewed close up, or when the beauty of the box is important in the display of the plant, the quality of the wood and the workmanship are all-important.

The above series of photos focuses on the craftsman-like detail built into the "Inlay," "Hexagonal," "Dowel Handle" and

A collection of corners

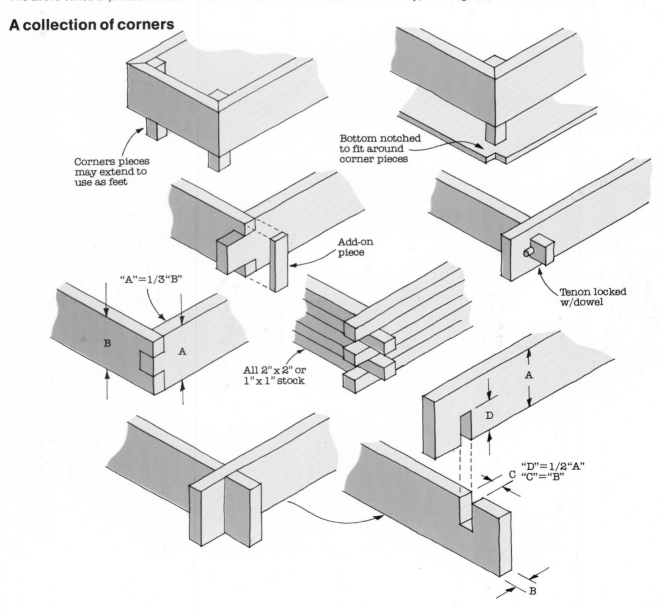

Corners pieces may extend to use as feet

Bottom notched to fit around corner pieces

Add-on piece

Tenon locked w/dowel

"A"=1/3"B"

B   A

All 2"x 2" or 1"x 1" stock

A

D

"D"=1/2"A"
"C"="B"

C

B

"Bonsai" boxes. Plans on pages 20 and 21. For other special corner treatments, see ideas below.

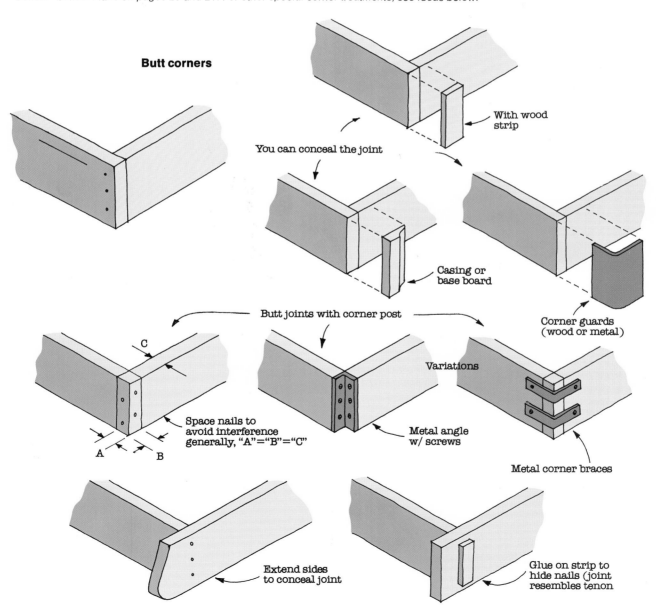

Butt corners

You can conceal the joint

With wood strip

Casing or base board

Corner guards (wood or metal)

Butt joints with corner post

C

Space nails to avoid interference generally, "A"="B"="C"

A   B

Variations

Metal angle w/ screws

Metal corner braces

Extend sides to conceal joint

Glue on strip to hide nails (joint resembles tenon

Craftsman's boxes

Craftsmanship takes many forms. One could be the many projects in this book. Another could be an exotic little project tackled just for the joy and challenge in doing it. The result would still hold a plant but the emphasis might be on a fancy hardwood, an intricate joint—a gem to display indoors or out, like a prize-winning flower.

The grooves for the inlaid box can be done with a crosscut saw, or a backsaw if you have one. Let the saw kerf determine the width of the groove. Make the layout and do the sawing carefully —speed is not important. Cut the inlay strips a bit thicker and wider than necessary. Then, use sandpaper to thin them for a snug fit, glue them in place, sand them flush after the glue is dry.

The hexagonal box requires accurate bevel-cuts. Saw the bevels on a long piece of wood and then cut off the lengths you need.

The dowel-handle box offers another challenge in precise angle-cutting. Do the ends first and then use them as a pattern to mark the correct angle on the sides. Hold the sides together when you drill the dowel holes. Cut the bottom to fit after all other parts are assembled.

The bonsai box is a mallet-and-chisel job, but if you do the drilling suggested in step 3, there'll be less waste to remove. Form the holes for the through-dowels by drilling from both sides of the stock.

Inlay box

Hexagonal box

Try to do the assembly work on all boxes by working only with glue. This will be easier if you have some clamps. If you use nails, be sure they are the finishing type you can set and conceal with wood dough.

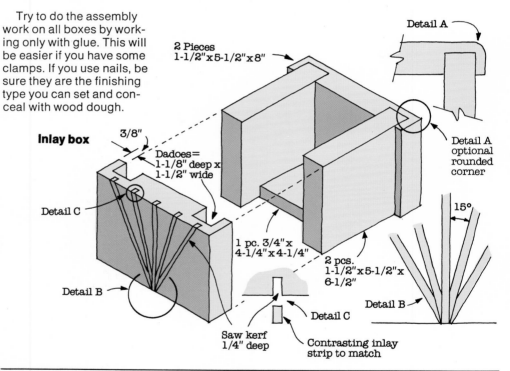

Inlay box

2 Pieces 1-1/2"x5-1/2"x8"

Detail A

3/8"

Dadoes= 1-1/8" deep x 1-1/2" wide

Detail C

Detail A optional rounded corner

1 pc. 3/4"x 4-1/4"x4-1/4"

2 pcs. 1-1/2"x5-1/2"x 6-1/2"

15°

Detail B

Detail B

Saw kerf 1/4" deep

Contrasting inlay strip to match

Detail C

Hexagonal box

Bevel angle=30°

2-1/2"

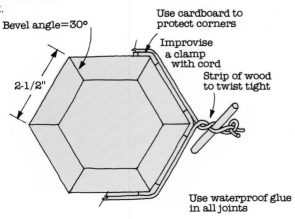

Use cardboard to protect corners

Improvise a clamp with cord

Strip of wood to twist tight

Use waterproof glue in all joints

Box sides require – 3 pcs. 3/4"x2-1/2"x4-3/4"
3 pcs. 3/4"x2-1/2"x4"

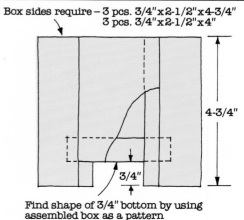

4-3/4"

3/4"

Find shape of 3/4" bottom by using assembled box as a pattern

Dowel box　　　　　*Bonsai box*

Dowel handle box

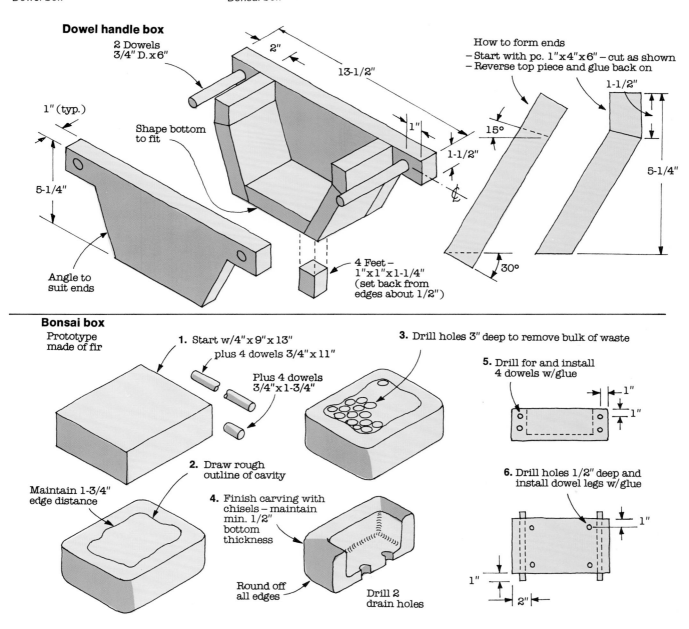

2 Dowels
3/4" D. x 6"

2"

13-1/2"

How to form ends
– Start with pc. 1"x4"x6" – cut as shown
– Reverse top piece and glue back on

1-1/2"

1" (typ.)

Shape bottom
to fit

1"

1-1/2"

15°

5-1/4"

5-1/4"

30°

Angle to
suit ends

4 Feet –
1"x1"x1-1/4"
(set back from
edges about 1/2")

Bonsai box

Prototype
made of fir

1. Start w/4"x9"x13"
plus 4 dowels 3/4"x11"

Plus 4 dowels
3/4"x1-3/4"

3. Drill holes 3" deep to remove bulk of waste

5. Drill for and install
4 dowels w/glue

1"

1"

Maintain 1-3/4"
edge distance

2. Draw rough
outline of cavity

4. Finish carving with
chisels – maintain
min. 1/2"
bottom
thickness

6. Drill holes 1/2" deep and
install dowel legs w/glue

1"

1"

2"

Round off
all edges

Drill 2
drain holes

This grape trellis design was adapted from those used in commercial vineyards.

Two grape plants are trained on the wire cross supports.

Trellises—with and without boxes

A trellis is usually for espaliering, but view the project and the plant together and think beyond support for vines or creeping plants. Think of windbreaks, privacy screens, wall decor—the project doesn't change, the application might.

Trellises can be heavy or light, simple or complex, self-contained or integrated with a box, stationary or movable, the standard pattern of open squares, an interesting weave or a dowel version. We show them all, so you can choose one to duplicate many times or make several types for contrast and suitability for different plants or locations.

Grape box

The box for our grape-espalier project is basically the same as the Apple box (next page) but employs an unusual trellis design very good for grapes. The main difference is the depth of the box and thickness of materials. Here, we work with a 2-inch *surfaced* stock, which nets at 1½-inches, as opposed to the full 2 inches of *unsurfaced* stock used for the Apple box.

Follow the box-assembly procedure for the Apple box —then cut the two vertical and four crossarm pieces for the trellis. Attach cross-arms to verticals and then hold assembled pieces in place while you drill holes for the carriage bolts.

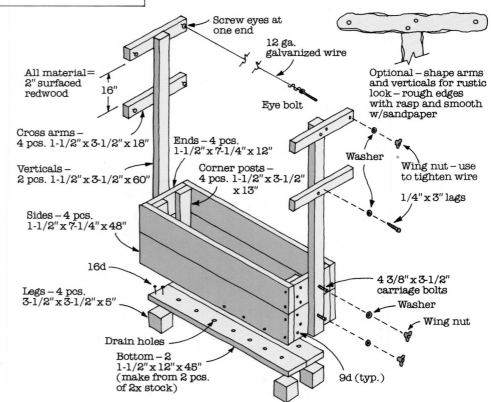

Screw eyes at one end

12 ga. galvanized wire

Eye bolt

All material = 2" surfaced redwood

16"

Cross arms – 4 pcs. 1-1/2" x 3-1/2" x 18"

Verticals – 2 pcs. 1-1/2" x 3-1/2" x 60"

Ends – 4 pcs. 1-1/2" x 7-1/4" x 12"

Corner posts – 4 pcs. 1-1/2" x 3-1/2" x 13"

Sides – 4 pcs. 1-1/2" x 7-1/4" x 48"

16d

Legs – 4 pcs. 3-1/2" x 3-1/2" x 5"

Drain holes

Bottom – 2 1-1/2" x 12" x 45" (make from 2 pcs. of 2x stock)

Optional – shape arms and verticals for rustic look – rough edges with rasp and smooth w/sandpaper

Washer

Wing nut – use to tighten wire

1/4" x 3" lags

4 3/8" x 3-1/2" carriage bolts

Washer

Wing nut

9d (typ.)

Basic box container is the same as the grape box. Trellis is designed for espaliering.

Apple box

A tree espalier, especially one in a container, is an interesting project that requires a trellis capable of supporting the lateral branches you allow to grow. Our apple box is large and sturdy enough for that purpose. The technique is to prune judiciously so the trunk of the tree follows the center vertical while selected laterals are forced along the horizontals.

Make the box by cutting ends, sides, and posts to length. Nail end pieces to the posts, and then add the sides. The posts are shorter than the box height by 2 inches—to allow for the thickness of the bottom. Cut the bottom piece to length and attach the feet before you add the bottom to the box.

View the trellis as a separate unit that you assemble before attaching it to the box. Cut all parts to length. Place horizontal pieces edge-to-edge so you can mark across them for notch locations. Form the notches by following the instructions on page 83. Size the notches so the horizontal pieces will slip easily over the verticals. If you are so precise that pieces must be hammered together, you will create stresses which will eventually cause splitting and cracking.

Assemble the trellis on a flat surface and add the screws called for at each crossing. When you attach the trellis to the box, locate the lag screws on each end-vertical so that one hits the corner post and the other penetrates the box-end. Use 4-inch lags on the center-vertical.

Big yields can be expected from a dwarf apple tree trained in this manner.

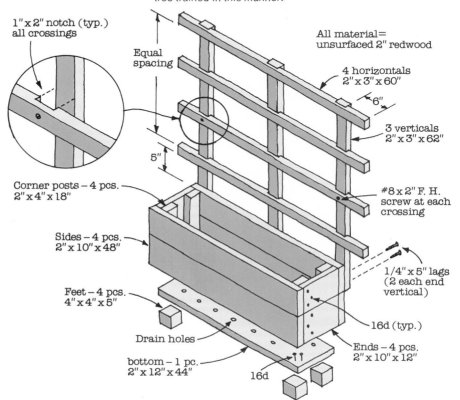

1" x 2" notch (typ.) all crossings

Equal spacing

5"

All material= unsurfaced 2" redwood

4 horizontals 2" x 3" x 60"

6"

3 verticals 2" x 3" x 62"

#8 x 2" F. H. screw at each crossing

Corner posts – 4 pcs. 2" x 4" x 18"

Sides – 4 pcs. 2" x 10" x 48"

Feet – 4 pcs. 4" x 4" x 5"

1/4" x 5" lags (2 each end vertical)

16d (typ.)

Drain holes

Ends – 4 pcs. 2" x 10" x 12"

bottom – 1 pc. 2" x 12" x 44"

16d

Container-grown grapes trained on trellises which seem to open their arms to the sun.

Vine-crop box

This handsome container with sloping sides offers the opportunity to use your sawing skills to cut compound-angle joints correctly (requires power cutoff saw). Each corner, as explained on pages 83 and 84, combines a miter and a bevel—not as simple as a butt or plain miter, but easy enough if you follow this procedure.

Place two pieces of 2x12 stock edge-to-edge. Mark two points 30 inches apart on the top edge and a center mark at 15″ on the bottom edge. Now, mark one point at 9″ to the left of

The unusual shape of this container is accentuated by the corresponding outward slope of the trellis.

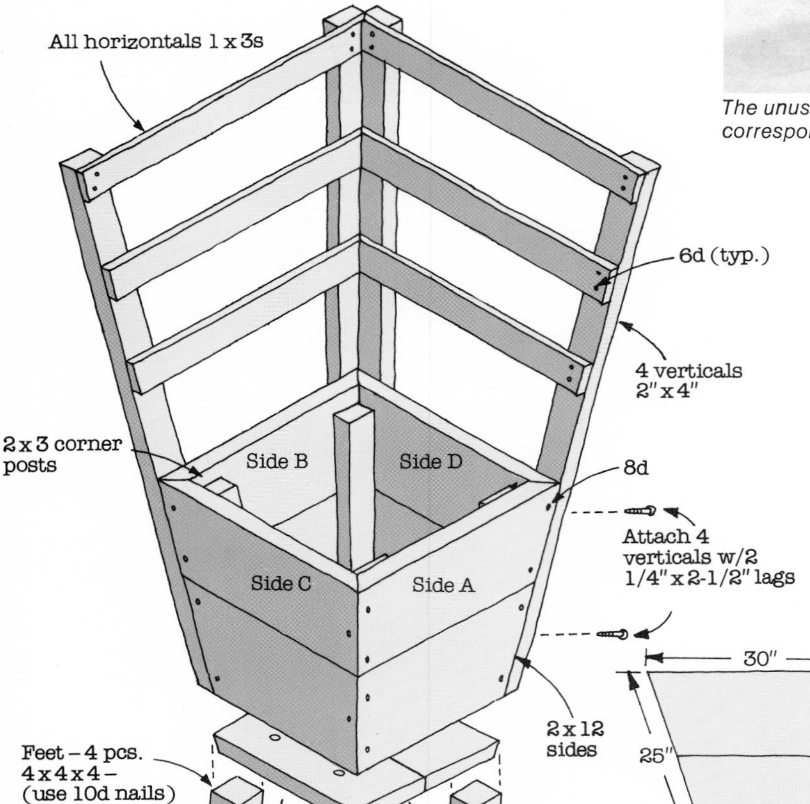

the center mark on the bottom and another 9″ to the right. Draw lines from 30″ marks to marks on bottom. Tilt saw to setting of 41¾° and make cuts on lines. This gives you the two pieces for one side of the box. Use these as patterns for other sides.

Nail corner posts into position on Sides "A" & "B." Form box by assembling with "C" & "D." Use box as pattern for bottom. Attach feet before you put bottom in place.

Put the trellis together by attaching the vertical 2x4s first, then the horizontal 1x3s. The latter nailing chores will be easier if you place the project on its side on a hard surface.

Provide drain holes. Treat the inside of the box by following the suggestions on pages 92 and 93.

Diagram labels:

All horizontals 1 x 3s

6d (typ.)

4 verticals 2″ x 4″

2 x 3 corner posts

Side B   Side D

8d

Attach 4 verticals w/2 1/4″ x 2-1/2″ lags

Side C   Side A

2 x 12 sides

Feet – 4 pcs. 4 x 4 x 4 – (use 10d nails)

Bottom – 2″ material

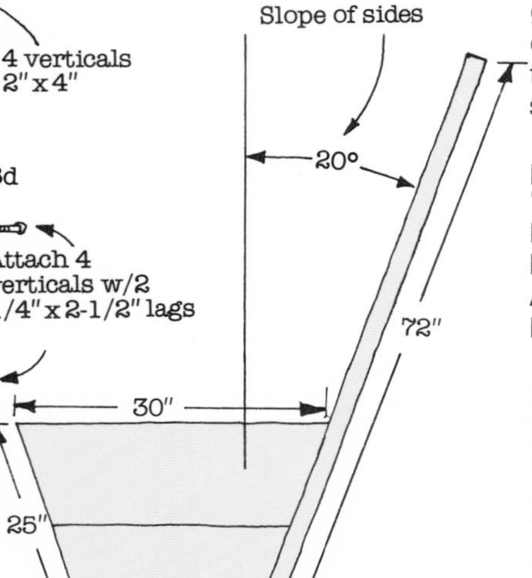

Slope of sides

20°

72″

30″

25″

18″

The trellis leans toward the outside wall which reflects extra heat to the plant.

Vines are supported on the trellis and melons on the movable shelves.

Watermelon box

This box with adjustable trellis is specially designed to provide adequate support for vines and fruit of watermelons but may be used for other vine crops such as squash or cantaloupes. Movable shelves support the fruit and may be placed wherever the plant decides to produce them.

If you check the drawing you will see that the sides and ends of the container can be assembled as units before being attached to each other. Be careful when placing the bottom cleats (C) and the vertical ones (F). The former are raised enough to allow room for the bottom; the others are situated so the container sides will be flush with the ends. Remember that the pieces designated as (A) are 2 inches longer than the other side pieces so they act as legs to elevate the

box above grade. You can substitute screws for nails if you wish, but in either case it's a good idea to coat all mating surfaces with waterproof glue. Cut the bottom to fit *after* the container parts have been assembled. Drill drain holes.

Cut all parts for the trellis to the lengths called out in the materials list. Do the assembly by attaching the top strip to the sides, then add the horizontal pieces and finally the vertical ones.

The carriage bolt and

wing nut are used so the trellis can pivot to a desirable position. The trellis can be supported by wall or fence. If not, cut suitable length of ¾- by 1½-inch stock that you can use as a prop.

Make two or three movable shelves to start. Hopefully, you'll need more.

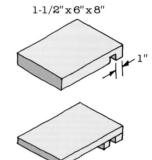

1-1/2" x 6" x 8"

1"

Make Shelves from 1½" stock with ¾" deep x ¾" wide groove — or ¾" stock with cleats

Box materials

A = 4 pcs. 2" x 2" x 16" rough redwood
B = 28 pcs. 2" x 2" x 14" rough redwood
C = 4 pcs. ¾" x 1½" x 32" surfaced redwood
D = 4 pcs. 2" x 2" x 20" rough redwood
E = 10 pcs. 2" x 2" x 16" rough redwood
F = 4 pcs. ¾" x 1½" x 13¼" surfaced redwood
G = 1 pc. ¾" x 12" x 32" Ext. Gr. Plywood

Trellis materials

H = 2 pcs. ¾" x 1½" x 48" surfaced redwood
I = 7 pcs. ¾" x 1½" x 36" surfaced redwood
J = 5 pcs. ¾" x 1½" x 45" surfaced redwood
K = 2   ¼" x 3½" carriage bolts
            w/washers and wing nuts

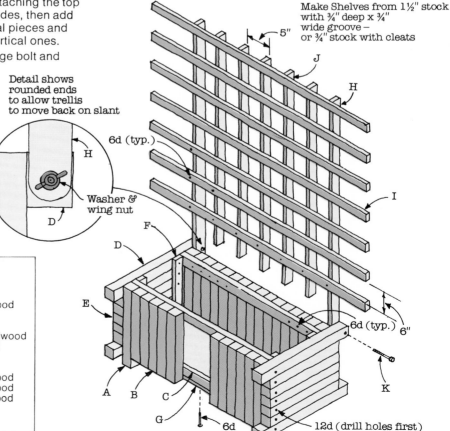

5"

J

H

6d (typ.)

Detail shows rounded ends to allow trellis to move back on slant

H

Washer & wing nut

D

F

D

E

A   B   C

G

6d

6d (typ.)   6"

I

K

12d (drill holes first)

The trellis' center vertical is optional. We constructed the boxes both ways.

A regal throne for a thriving tomato plant.

Tomato Box

Before constructing this project, check the drawing and see how the verticals of the trellis are designed as part of the box. Cut all side pieces to length and assemble them to the cleats, but provide for two things—an opening on the back panel so the center trellis-vertical will fit in; and space below bottom cleats so the ¾"-inch plywood bottom can be inset.

Next step is to cut all parts for the trellis. Cut the notches by working with a dado assembly on a table saw or by following the hand tool instructions on page 91. Assemble the trellis by driving the screws called for at each crossing.

Attach the front panel to the front corners, add the side panels, and then the back panel *and* trellis. In

each case, three screws are used on adjacent sides of each corner. Secure the center trellis-vertical by nailing through the back cleats.

Size the bottom and drill through it for drain holes. Place the project flat, on the trellis, and attach the bottom by driving nails along its perimeter into all bottom cleats.

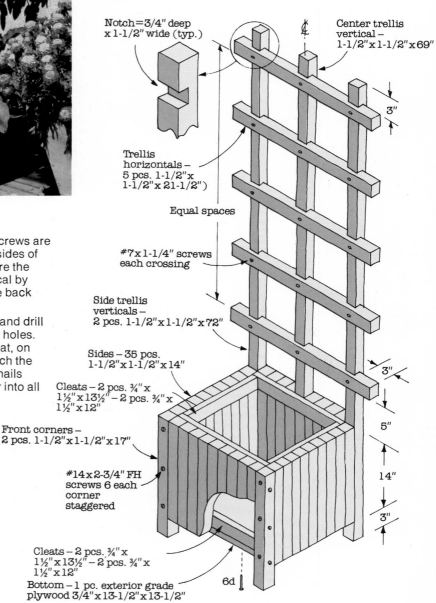

Notch=3/4" deep x 1-1/2" wide (typ.)

Center trellis vertical – 1-1/2"x1-1/2"x69"

3"

Trellis horizontals – 5 pcs. 1-1/2"x 1-1/2"x 21-1/2")

Equal spaces

#7x1-1/4" screws each crossing

Side trellis verticals – 2 pcs. 1-1/2"x1-1/2"x72"

Sides – 35 pcs. 1-1/2"x1-1/2"x14"

Cleats – 2 pcs. ¾" x 1½"x13½" – 2 pcs. ¾" x 1½"x12"

Front corners – 2 pcs. 1-1/2"x1-1/2"x17"

#14x2-3/4" FH screws 6 each corner staggered

3"

5"

14"

3"

Cleats – 2 pcs. ¾" x 1½"x13½" – 2 pcs. ¾" x 1½"x12"

Bottom – 1 pc. exterior grade plywood 3/4"x13-1/2"x13-1/2"

6d

Designed for growing vine crops vertically, this A-frame trellis has lemon cucumbers on one side and beans on the other.

For the young adventurer it's a "tunnel of beans and cukes"— easy picking for a kid-sized reach.

A-frame Trellis

The A-frame trellis may be used with two containers or as a freestanding unit to support vine plants sowed directly in the ground. The hinge arrangement at the top provides for span and height adjustments so you have considerable leeway when spacing containers or seed rows. To stir your imagination, consider that the project, when not used as an "A," may be opened completely and braced vertically to provide a trellis 4½' high by 12' long.

Cut all parts for the trellis to correct length. Do the assembly by nailing the legs (6-foot pieces) to all the horizontal strips and then adding the verticals. Cut one piece of material 6-inches long and use it as a gauge for correct spacing. The 4d nails called for are adequate but if you want more strength use 6d nails and clinch them on the back. Use 2-inch brass hinges with brass screws. Place one at each end and a third one in the center.

The containers shown are butt-jointed with glue and 7d nails. Add the bottom by nailing from the outside. The feet are 4-inch lengths cut from 4- x 4-inch stock, secured with glue and nails driven from the inside of the container. The cap strips are optional but add enough to the appearance of the project to make the addition worthwhile.

Don't neglect to provide drain holes.

Trellis is a separate unit. It may be used with a variety of containers or separately for ground plantings.

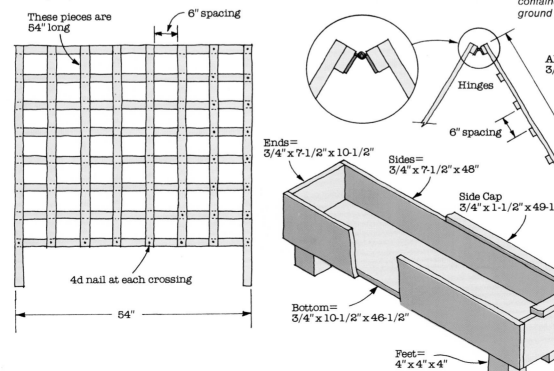

These pieces are 54" long

6" spacing

4d nail at each crossing

54"

Hinges

All material 3/4" x 1-1/2"

6" spacing

72"

Ends= 3/4" x 7-1/2" x 10-1/2"

Sides= 3/4" x 7-1/2" x 48"

Side Cap 3/4" x 1-1/2" x 49-1/2"

Bottom= 3/4" x 10-1/2" x 46-1/2"

End cap 3/4" x 1-1/2" x 13-1/2"

Feet= 4" x 4" x 4"

Adjustable trellis made with 1 x 1's can be widened to train two pots of tomato plants.

. . . or easily adjusted for one pot in a smaller space.

Folding Trellis

The folding trellis works like an accordion, so its height and width can be adjusted for various situations. The critical phase of the construction is the spacing of the pivot holes. These must be accurate on each piece for the trellis to open and close smoothly. Do a careful layout on one piece and use it as a pattern to drill others individually or by stacking them. The slot in the end posts is necessary so the terminal points on the trellis can move freely when you are making a size adjustment.

The concept permits the use of any size of material. You can, for example, work with ¾-inch stock if you need more rigidity than lath provides. If you do make a change, be sure to purchase cotter pins and carriage bolts that are long enough for the job.

Two folding trellises constructed with lath were used for this row of container tomatoes.

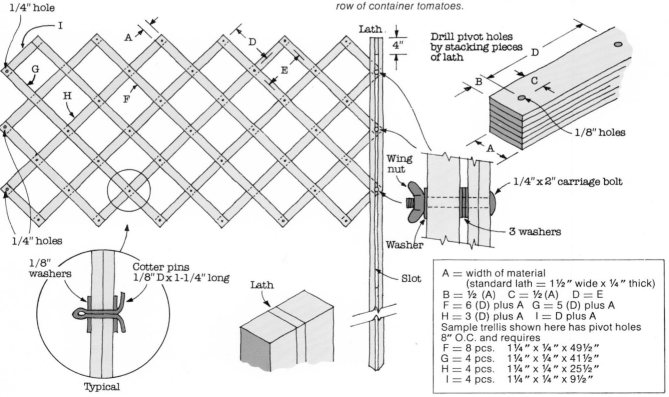

A = width of material
(standard lath = 1½″ wide x ¼″ thick)
B = ½ (A)   C = ½ (A)   D = E
F = 6 (D) plus A   G = 5 (D) plus A
H = 3 (D) plus A   I = D plus A
Sample trellis shown here has pivot holes 8″ O.C. and requires
F = 8 pcs.   1¼″ x ¼″ x 49½″
G = 4 pcs.   1¼″ x ¼″ x 41½″
H = 4 pcs.   1¼″ x ¼″ x 25½″
I = 4 pcs.   1¼″ x ¼″ x 9½″

Interwoven lath panels and portable posts in clay pots. Three panels joined together serve as a trellis for tomato plants grown in 5-gallon cans. Low hide-a-can panel in front (see page 11) gives a raised-bed effect.

Interwoven Trellis and Portable Posts

These trellises can be used individually, or combined as screens for wide areas, or to provide espalier support for lines of plants in pots or in the ground. They can move anywhere when mounted on portable posts.

You can make the grooved frames with standard materials. Or, you can take 1½ x 2½-inch stock and run a ½-inch-wide by 1-inch-deep groove down the center of it with a table saw. Don't make the grooves narrower because you'll need the width when you weave the lath—or overlay the strips—whichever you decide to do.

The best procedure is to assemble three sides of the frame, install the lath, and add the fourth frame piece. Lath is easier to weave if you soak it first. Plan for openings 6 to 10 inches square. Woven strips will be tight enough so you won't need fasteners where they cross or end in grooves. Overlaid strips need a nail at each crossing point.

The portable posts are 2 x 4s imbedded in concrete in 10-inch clay pots. Remove the bottom of pot by using a carbide-tipped blade in a saber saw or with a tungsten-carbide rasp. Drive a few 16d nails part way into the 2 x 4 to serve as wood-to-concrete anchors.

Do the job on level ground and brace posts in true vertical position until concrete sets.

Attach the trellises to the posts with carriage bolts and wing nuts. If you make the posts longer than you need for the immediate application you will be able to raise or lower the trellis at will merely by drilling new holes for the carriage bolts.

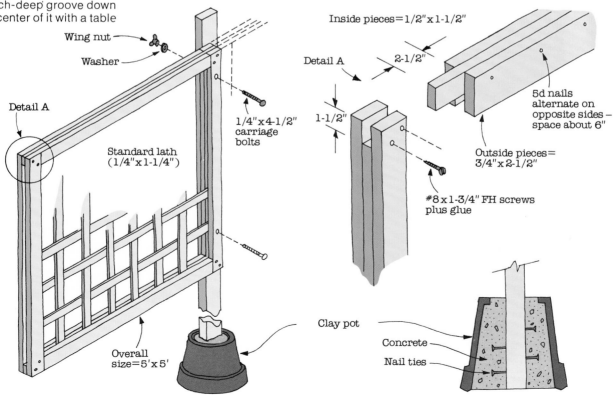

Inside pieces = 1/2" x 1-1/2"

Detail A

2-1/2"

1-1/2"

5d nails alternate on opposite sides – space about 6"

Outside pieces = 3/4" x 2-1/2"

#8 x 1-3/4" FH screws plus glue

Wing nut

Washer

Detail A

1/4" x 4-1/2" carriage bolts

Standard lath (1/4" x 1-1/4")

Overall size = 5' x 5'

Clay pot

Concrete

Nail ties

A simple ladder-type trellis made from dowels and attached to rafters under eaves. Soon the vine will cover it and make this a wall of flowers.

Dowel trellis

Trellises vary in design and application. Ladder types, made with standard dowels of various diameters, are a nice change of pace from lath types in appearance and in construction procedures. Dowel diameters run from ⅛ inch to over 1 inch so the trellises can be light or heavy, depending on the plant you wish to support. Posts can be 2 x 2, 2 x 3, or 2 x 4 stock.

The standard dowel length is three feet. Bear this in mind when you design so you can avoid waste.

In all situations, hold, or preferably, clamp the posts together so you can drill mating dowel holes through both at the same time.

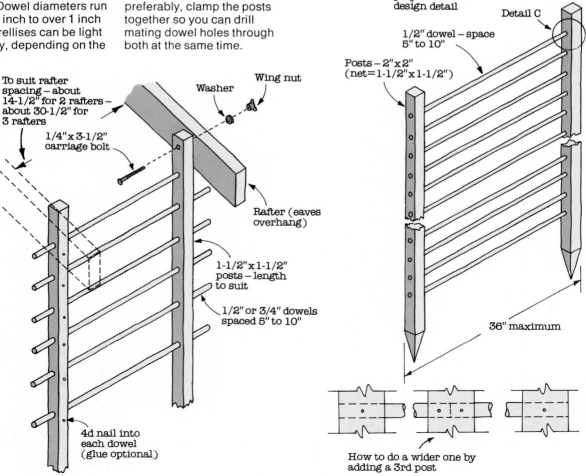

To suit rafter spacing – about 14-1/2" for 2 rafters – about 30-1/2" for 3 rafters

Washer

Wing nut

1/4"x3-1/2" carriage bolt

Rafter (eaves overhang)

1-1/2"x1-1/2" posts – length to suit

1/2" or 3/4" dowels spaced 5" to 10"

4d nail into each dowel (glue optional)

Detail C

Dowel may project as design detail

4d nail

Detail C

1/2" dowel – space 5" to 10"

Posts – 2"x2" (net=1-1/2"x1-1/2")

36" maximum

How to do a wider one by adding a 3rd post

Nobody ever used this garage door, so we decided to trellis it. In stages it is becoming a door of 'Heavenly Blue' morning glories.

Door trellis

This trellis was sized to cover an unused garage door but similar ones can be set up on posts or hung on a house wall or fence. The framing technique is flexible so you can work with materials of your choice. The front piece can be 1 x 3 material, the back 1 x 2..

Cut the laths to fit between the back pieces and hold them in place with 2d nails driven from the back so they will not be visible. Overlay the diamond shapes on the horizontal laths and secure them with nails at each crossing point.

Use two or three nails on each side, toe nailed into the jambs, to hold the trellis in a doorway. Sketches below show various methods you can use to hang trellises.

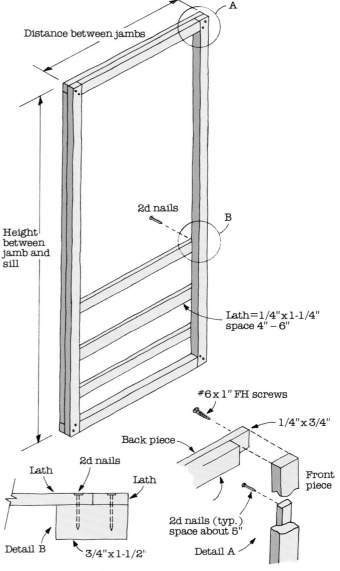

Distance between jambs

A

2d nails

B

Height between jamb and sill

Lath=1/4"x1-1/4" space 4" – 6"

#6 x 1" FH screws

1/4" x 3/4"

Back piece

Front piece

2d nails (typ.) space about 5"

Detail A

Lath   2d nails   Lath

Detail B   3/4"x1-1/2"

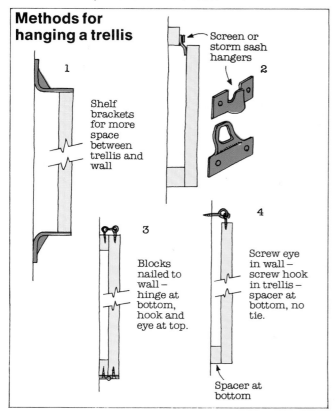

Methods for hanging a trellis

1 Shelf brackets for more space between trellis and wall

2 Screen or storm sash hangers

3 Blocks nailed to wall – hinge at bottom, hook and eye at top.

4 Screw eye in wall – screw hook in trellis – spacer at bottom, no tie.

Spacer at bottom

The folding screen can be used as a patio divider. Double-action hinges give it flexibility.

Free-standing Screen Trellis

Why not move the classic folding screen, traditionally an indoor device, outdoors? Readily available, double-action hinges (ask for "folding-screen hinges") make the project flexible enough so it can be organized to surround a container, be used as a windscreen, or set up as a temporary espalier.

You can make a sturdy frame by assembling standard-size pieces of wood, as shown in the details on page 33 or, if you work with a table saw, by running a ½-inch-wide by 1-inch-deep groove down the center of 1½ x 2½-inch stock. If you make the side pieces long enough they will serve as legs to elevate the lattice portion above grade. This is not a bad idea, especially if you plan to use the screen to espalier plants in the ground.

Our prototypes have a limited weave. The first two horizontal pieces go over the vertical ones, the next two go behind, and so on. You can, of course, simply overlay all lath pieces and use a small nail at each crossing.

The usual folding screen has three panels but there's no reason why you can't add a fourth if you wish.

Double-action hinges are sold in pairs but buy enough so you can use *three* hinges on each section of the screen. This will greatly counteract any tendency of the sections to distort.

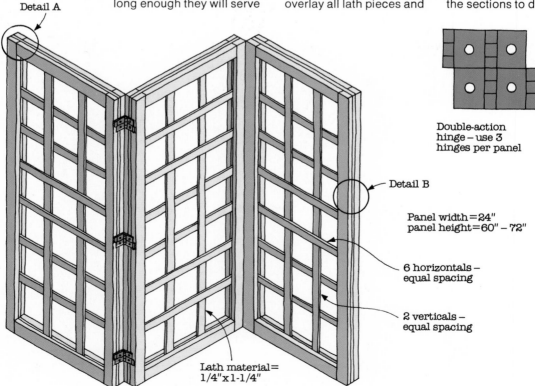

Detail A

Double-action hinge – use 3 hinges per panel

Detail B

Panel width = 24"
panel height = 60" – 72"

6 horizontals –
equal spacing

2 verticals –
equal spacing

Lath material =
1/4" x 1-1/4"

A cheesecloth backing added on each panel reflects sunlight and blocks wind while creating a delightful dining atmosphere.

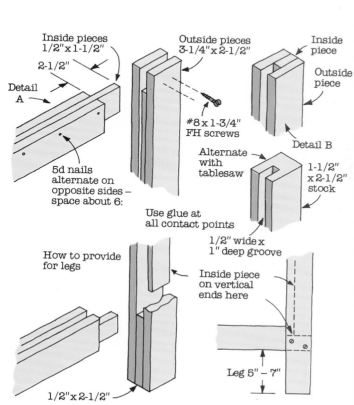

Inside pieces 1/2" x 1-1/2"

2-1/2"

Detail A

5d nails alternate on opposite sides – space about 6:

Outside pieces 3-1/4" x 2-1/2"

#8 x 1-3/4" FH screws

Alternate with tablesaw

Inside piece

Outside piece

Detail B

1-1/2" x 2-1/2" stock

Use glue at all contact points

1/2" wide x 1" deep groove

How to provide for legs

Inside piece on vertical ends here

1/2" x 2-1/2"

Leg 5" – 7"

The screen used to warm plants in early season

Raised beds—on the ground and in the air

Many a gardener finds himself working with soil that won't support a vegetable garden.

In such problem situations, growing plants above the soil in a raised bed is the best answer.

One of the primary advantages of the raised bed is that the gardener has a choice when deciding what kind of soil he wants to garden in. When the bed is filled with a light-weight soil mix rich in organic matter the gardener has a very efficient vegetable growing factory.

If the mixture is light-weight, drainage through the soil is good and with soil raised above ground level, drainage away from the bed is possible. This is seen by many gardeners as a big advantage because in a wet, cool spring the soil in the raised bed will warm up and be ready to plant weeks before regular garden soil can be seeded or worked.

If the raised bed is accessible from both sides, a width of 6 feet is practical. Planting, weeding and harvesting can be handled without walking in the bed. If the raised bed is alongside a fence or for any reason accessible from only one side, make the width 3 to 4'. The height of the bed should be at least 12" above the soil. If the raised bed is built 16" high and capped with 2 x 6" boards, you can sit while you weed.

Raised bed with seat adds comfort to good gardening.

Raised Beds

Raised beds are no more than large, bottomless containers. The sides and ends of the box can be wood of any thickness, 1-inch or 2-inch material, railroad ties or old telephone poles, brick or concrete. The beds illustrated here are built of two-inch-thick material. They can be 6 to 15 inches high, secured with lag bolts to corner posts, buried or cut at grade. Projects as large as 4 x 10 feet can be installed with corner posts only. If larger, add intermediate posts for additional bracing, and bury them because they will not pro-

vide lateral support if attached only to the side boards.

After building and placing the container, you may want to add a cap to improve appearance. Use 2-inch dressed stock for this and secure to the side boards with 16d nails. Either miter or butt the corners. A seat along one or more sides is a practical addition. Check details in the drawings for how-to specifics.

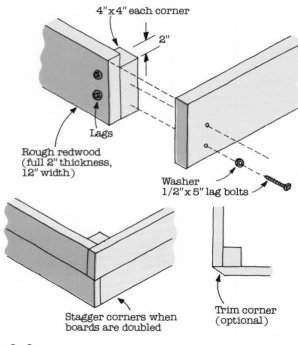

4"x4" each corner
2"
Lags
Rough redwood
(full 2" thickness,
12" width)
Washer
1/2"x 5" lag bolts

Stagger corners when boards are doubled

Trim corner (optional)

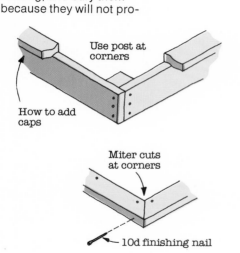

Use post at corners

How to add caps

Miter cuts at corners

10d finishing nail

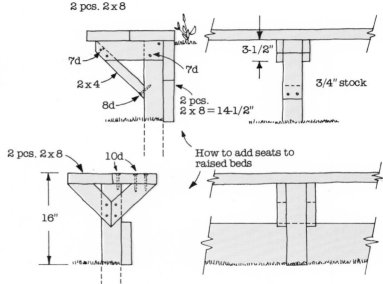

2 pcs. 2 x 8
7d
7d
3-1/2"
2 x 4
3/4" stock
8d
2 pcs.
2 x 8 = 14-1/2"

2 pcs. 2 x 8
10d
16"

How to add seats to raised beds

Closeup of seat construction.

A drip irrigation system installed in bed.

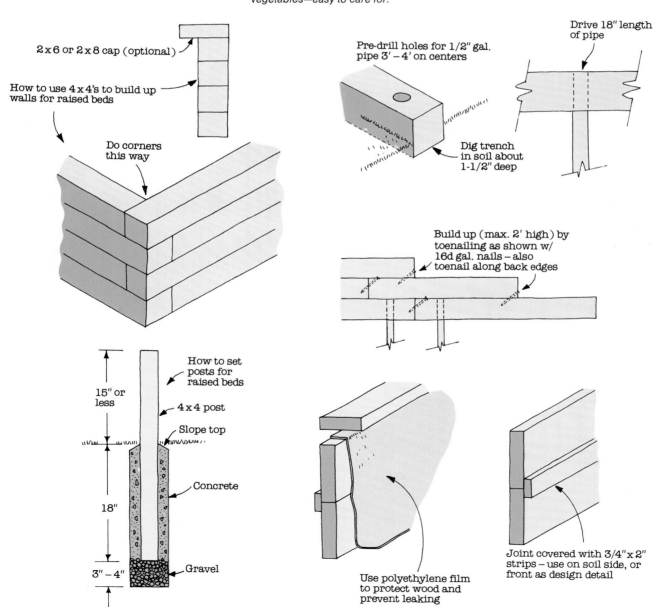

The project blossoms with plantings of dwarf flowers mixed with vegetables—easy to care for.

2 x 6 or 2 x 8 cap (optional)

How to use 4 x 4's to build up walls for raised beds

Do corners this way

Pre-drill holes for 1/2" gal. pipe 3' – 4' on centers

Dig trench in soil about 1-1/2" deep

Drive 18" length of pipe

Build up (max. 2' high) by toenailing as shown w/ 16d gal. nails – also toenail along back edges

How to set posts for raised beds

15" or less

4 x 4 post

Slope top

Concrete

18"

3" – 4"

Gravel

Use polyethylene film to protect wood and prevent leaking

Joint covered with 3/4"x 2" strips – use on soil side, or front as design detail

Gardening is easy on the back in this waist high raised bed— and you won't miss the sights along the way.

Putterer's Garden

The putterer's garden project offers control and convenience—control over the soil, and convenience in terms of height and size. Shapes can be square or rectangular, even designed as modules and arranged with aisles for easy access. You can, if you wish, utilize the underspace by attaching a plywood or board-covered 2 x 4 frame to the legs. (If you do the latter, attach a sheet of plastic to the underside of the con-

Fine screen stapled over drainage hole, keeps soil in.

Sloping panel keeps drainage off lower storage shelf.

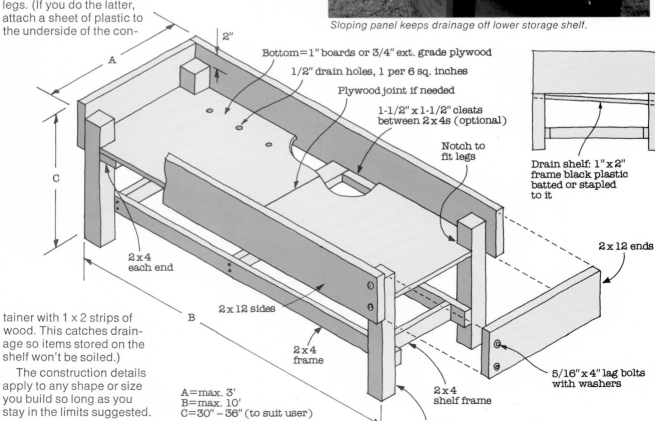

2"

A

C

B

2 x 4
each end

2 x 12 sides

2 x 4
frame

Bottom=1" boards or 3/4" ext. grade plywood

1/2" drain holes, 1 per 6 sq. inches

Plywood joint if needed

1-1/2" x 1-1/2" cleats
between 2 x 4s (optional)

Notch to
fit legs

Drain shelf: 1" x 2"
frame black plastic
batted or stapled
to it

2 x 12 ends

5/16" x 4" lag bolts
with washers

2 x 4
shelf frame

4 x 4 legs

tainer with 1 x 2 strips of wood. This catches drainage so items stored on the shelf won't be soiled.)

The construction details apply to any shape or size you build so long as you stay in the limits suggested.

A=max. 3'
B=max. 10'
C=30" – 36" (to suit user)

A curved raised bed using the kerfed-board technique.

Kerfed-board Raised Bed

If you wish to bend wood and can't steam it, kerf it! The technique works on any stock thickness and is especially effective for the less demanding turns you're likely to encounter in garden woodworking. Although deep, closely spaced kerfs will permit sharp bends, it's always best to limit the number of kerfs so the job can be done in minimum time and without weakening the wood excessively.

Keep kerf depth to about three quarters of the stock thickness. Use 2-inch spacing to start. If this proves inadequate for the bend, add additional kerfs between those already formed. Wetting the unkerfed surface of the board helps.

The gauge shown in the sketch lets you make the cuts faster and will keep the kerfs parallel. To use it, you must cut the first few kerfs freehand. Then work with the gauge as shown in the detail.

A simple gauge guides the saw to equal spacing.

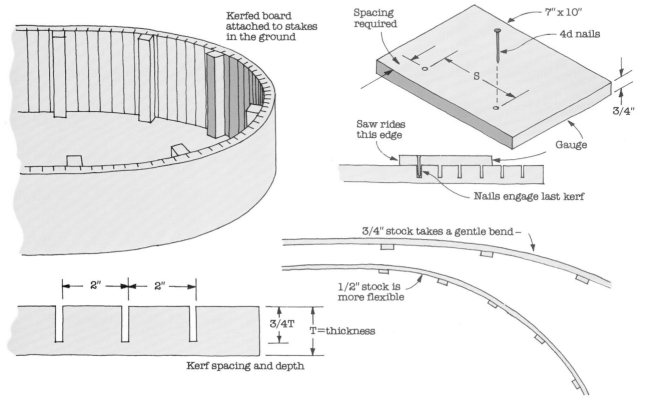

Kerfed board attached to stakes in the ground

Spacing required

7" x 10"

4d nails

S

3/4"

Gauge

Saw rides this edge

Nails engage last kerf

3/4" stock takes a gentle bend

1/2" stock is more flexible

2" 2"

3/4T

T=thickness

Kerf spacing and depth

Our "duckboards" serve many functions

The original duckboard was used as a raised platform or floor over a muddy or wet area—a concept you can still put to use. But why not try some of the other useful duckboard ideas shown here and on the following pages? You'll find that each one has a lot of potential for any project requiring a flat surface.

Just bear in mind that two areas of construction depend on how you're going to use the project. One is the spacing between boards. For a bench or table, three-quarter-inch spacing is about maximum. If the project is intended for plant display, spacing is not critical as there are few pots or containers that can't span several inches.

The second point to consider is the understructure, If it is to be only temporary, use concrete blocks, large flue tiles, short lengths of telephone pole, or heavy timbers. Concrete blocks come in 8x8x16-inch sizes, and smaller. Flue tiles are available in a range of dimensions. Poles and timbers can be cut to suit your specifications. With this choice of ready-made pieces, you can set your duckboard at almost any height you want.

Duckboards keep a muddy area dry.

A clean spot to step when using hose faucet.

Duckboards

Duckboards placed under or around outdoor faucets provide clean footing and a platform on which you can coil garden hose. Two good designs for the application are the grid type and the doweled version. Either one can be made with an opening just by using shorter inside pieces. Be sure to provide enough room for the project to pass easily over the faucet.

The units must resist considerable wetting and probably soil contact, so work with heart grades of redwood, cypress, or cedar, or apply generous amounts of preservative to the wood before setting the projects in place. Set them directly on grade, or excavate so the duckboard will be flush. In the latter situation, excavate deep enough so you can rest the unit on a 3- or 4-inch layer of gravel.

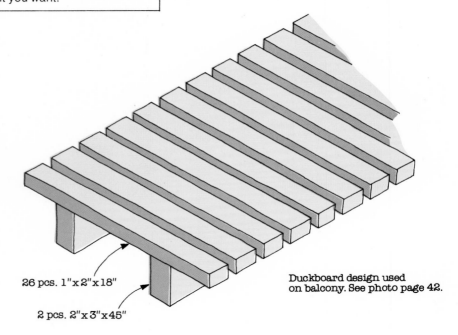

26 pcs. 1"x 2"x 18"

2 pcs. 2"x 3"x 45"

Duckboard design used on balcony. See photo page 42.

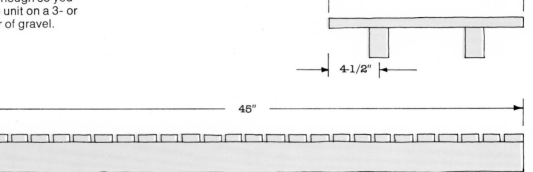

18"

4-1/2"

45"

On temporary supports, this portable duckboard serves as garden picnic table.

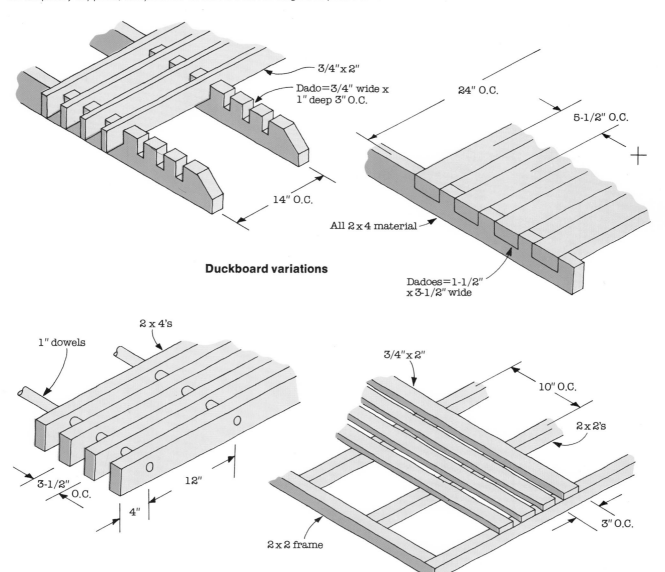

3/4" x 2"

Dado=3/4" wide x
1" deep 3" O.C.

14" O.C.

24" O.C.

5-1/2" O.C.

All 2 x 4 material

Dadoes=1-1/2"
x 3-1/2" wide

Duckboard variations

1" dowels

2 x 4's

3-1/2"
O.C.

12"

4"

3/4" x 2"

10" O.C.

2 x 2's

2 x 2 frame

3" O.C.

Versatile duckboards surround stationary deck to increase area or provide seating when raised.

Duckboards and a deck

The perimeter sections of the grade-level deck are movable duckboards! By using one, two, or more concrete blocks as legs, the duckboards serve as benches, plant-display platforms, even as buffet tables.

The flexibility is intriguing since the entire perimeter of the deck can function in any one of the above capacities, or the duckboards can be set at various heights to serve all purposes. Concrete blocks are suggested as pedestals because they are easy to obtain and use, but short lengths of telephone pole or similar items are as practical if available. Whatever you use, be sure the duckboards are stable at the new height.

The layout shown is just an example of how the deck should be planned. Stay with the 2-foot duckboard width but change lengths to suit your requirements. Design them as modular units—the perimeter pattern will be attractive, and construction/cutting will be easier. Don't make any duckboard so short that it becomes impractical for other purposes, or so long that it will be a chore to lift.

The deck is designed so you can erect it on the existing grade—or at grade level by removing the top 3-inches of soil. In the latter case, install staked, 2x4, border headers to define the site. Perimeter areas require an additional half inch of excavation so the duckboards will be flush with the fixed deck. Grade the area for a slight slope toward a drainage point and then tamp it and cover it with sheet plastic.

Choice of wood for the project is a personal thing. The fixed area of the prototype is Douglas fir — the duckboards were made with a construction-grade redwood. The project is easier to do if you work with better grades of wood, especially when doing the grid-type duckboards because they require much nailing.

The deck boards are nailed to 2x6 sleepers which sit directly on the plastic. Treating the sleepers with a preservative is a good "extra". The top boards can be butted—or separated just enough for drainage by using the spacing gauge shown in the sketch. Be sure all boards are cut to correct length and that all corners are square.

Decide on which of the two methods shown will be used for the assembly of duckboards.

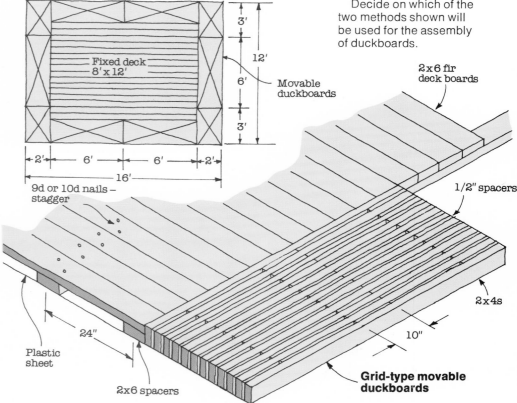

Grid-type movable duckboards

The deck becomes a gathering place for family and friends.

For extra seating, and plant display, raise portions of the duckboard and support with wood blocks.

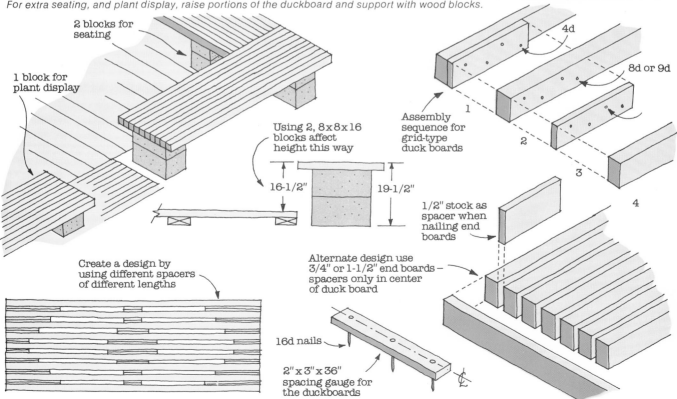

2 blocks for seating

1 block for plant display

Using 2, 8 x 8 x 16 blocks affect height this way

16-1/2"   19-1/2"

Assembly sequence for grid-type duck boards

4d

8d or 9d

1

2

3

4

1/2" stock as spacer when nailing end boards

Alternate design use 3/4" or 1-1/2" end boards – spacers only in center of duck board

Create a design by using different spacers of different lengths

16d nails

2" x 3" x 36" spacing gauge for the duckboards

Permanent supports were added to a duckboard for plant display.

Used as a balcony organizer, duckboards provide good drainage when plants are watered.

A variation of the leg supports.

For details on building this duckboard design. See page 38.

Duckboard Supports

In addition to using available materials, you can make supports for duckboards so they can be used as tables, benches, or plant displays. Two of the ideas shown here are basic bench-leg assemblies, each one attached to the slab with lag bolts. These are permanent set-ups, even though you can separate the slab from the legs by removing the lags. The stretchers shown are optional but they help prevent lateral sway, which can occur after a bench has been in use outdoors for a period of time.

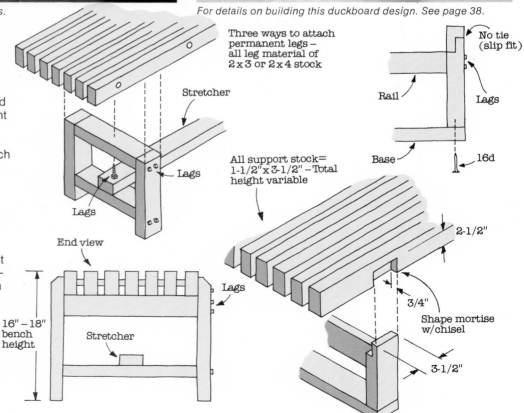

Stretcher

Three ways to attach permanent legs — all leg material of 2 x 3 or 2 x 4 stock

Lags

Lags

No tie (slip fit)

Rail

Lags

Base

16d

All support stock = 1-1/2" x 3-1/2" — Total height variable

Lags

End view

16" – 18" bench height

Stretcher

2-1/2"

3/4"

Shape mortise w/chisel

3-1/2"

Low duckboard table with center cut out for hibachi; can also be used as plant display.

Place pillows around it, serve hot hors d'oeuvres or a full meal.

Hibachi Table

This low table takes its hibachi to heart.

Assemble the slab by following the DECK-TOP BENCH instructions on page 61. The opening for the hibachi can be cut out after the slab is complete but it's wiser to provide for it right off. Measure the width, length, and depth of the hibachi and make a butt-jointed, open-top box for it. Use ¾-inch redwood and be sure to allow for the ¼-inch-thick asbestos

lining. Don't be too precise—air space around the hibachi is okay. Size the width of the box so you won't have to notch any of the slab pieces. Now you can assemble the slab with center pieces cut short to accommodate the box.

Cut all leg pieces to length and mark leg-dowel locations on one of the spacers. Drill pilot holes through this and use it as a pattern to mark other spacers. Be careful here

because the dowel must hit the center of two of the slab pieces (see end view). Do not use glue or fasteners when you assemble the legs and when you attach them to the slab—they are removable so table height is adjustable.

Put the hibachi box in place by nailing through its sides into the slab pieces. Attach the asbestos lining with two or three screws

through each piece. Do not attempt to cut asbestos sheets with conventional woodworking saws. You can use a masonry blade or a suitable abrasive disc in a portable saw if you cut slowly.

Last step is to attach the metal trim shown in the detail.

Even though the hibachi box is well fireproofed, never leave the unit unattended while it contains burning coals. Play it safe when you are through—remove the unit.

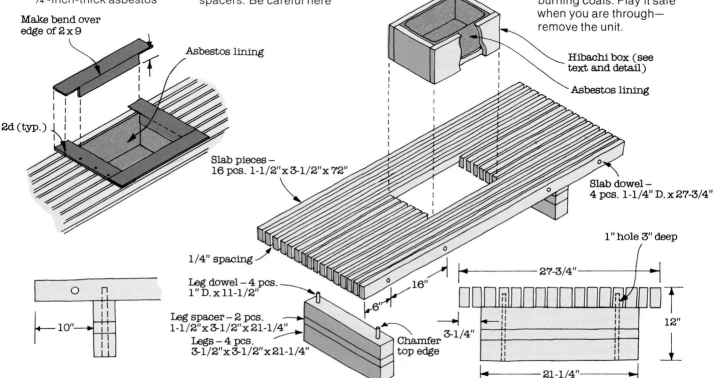

Make bend over edge of 2 x 9

Asbestos lining

2d (typ.)

Hibachi box (see text and detail)

Asbestos lining

Slab pieces —
16 pcs. 1-1/2" x 3-1/2" x 72"

Slab dowel —
4 pcs. 1-1/4" D. x 27-3/4"

1/4" spacing

1" hole 3" deep

10"

Leg dowel — 4 pcs.
1" D. x 11-1/2"

Leg spacer – 2 pcs.
1-1/2" x 3-1/2" x 21-1/4"

Legs – 4 pcs.
3-1/2" x 3-1/2" x 21-1/4"

Chamfer top edge

16"

6"

3-1/4"

27-3/4"

12"

21-1/4"

The lounge is dimensioned so you can use a standard 24-inch by 70-inch pad.

Deck Lounge

The fasteners you use to assemble the components of the lounge will affect its appearance. Galvanized box nails are the fastest way to go but may be visually distracting. Finishing nails can be hidden if you set them and then fill the holes with a wood dough.

The strongest and most professional method is to use wood screws, driven through counterbored holes and concealed with wooden plugs. Check the information on screws on page 87 for how this is done. In any case, use waterproof glue in all joints.

Start construction by assembling the base—parts A and B. Cut all the deck pieces to length and place them on the frame so you have equal projection on sides and ends. Remove the four pieces that belong to the tiltable back and then secure the others to the frame using four fasteners per board. Make a subassembly of the remaining four pieces and the two cleats—part E. Be sure these are placed so they clear the sides and the back end of the frame when the back is in horizontal position.

Install the hinges and then turn the project over and mark the correct location of part C. Its position should be low enough to provide clearance for the cleats. After part C is set, you can tilt the back to the angle that suits you and cut the braces—part F—to fit. Drill holes through the braces and the cleats for the carriage bolts and then add the crossbrace—part G.

The details in the drawing show how you can add legs if you wish to increase the height of the lounge, and how you can install a partial bottom so the back end of the lounge may be used for storage of towels and such. If you add legs, use carriage bolts to attach them. The storage compartment pieces can be secured with finishing nails driven from the outside of the base.

Two screen door pulls attached to one side of the frame will serve nicely as handles and can also be used to hang the lounge on a fence or inside wall of a garage or carport.

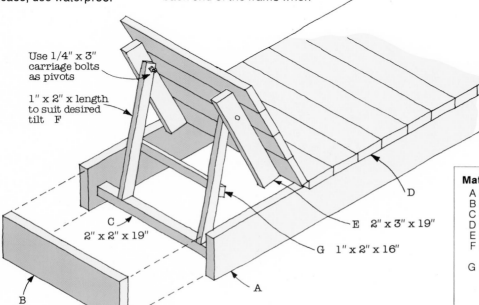

Use 1/4" x 3" carriage bolts as pivots

1" x 2" x length to suit desired tilt   F

C
2" x 2" x 19"

B

E   2" x 3" x 19"

G   1" x 2" x 16"

D

A

Materials
A = 2 pcs. 2" x 8" x 70"
B = 2 pcs. 2" x 8" x 19"
C = 1 pc. 2" x 2" x 19"
D = 13 pcs. 2" x 6" x 24"
E = 2 pcs. 2" x 3" x 19"
F = 2 pcs. 1" x 2" x optional
　　　(to suit back slant desired)
G = 1 pc.1" x 2" x 16"

1 pair 3" butt hinges
2¼" x 3" carriage bolts .w/nuts
　　and washers
Use kiln dried clear redwood
　　or ponderosa pine

Great for sunning, with or without a pad. Tilt the back up and you can read in comfort.

The tilting back allows easy access to storage area.

Add the partial bottom to provide for storage.

Hinge (2 Req.)

2" x 6" x 24"

2" x 8" x 70"

2" x 8" x 19"

Notched 2 x 4

or 1" material
added to 2 x 4

How to
add legs

Add a bottom:
Use exterior
Grade Fir
Plywood

3/4" x 7-1/2" x 19"

3/4" x 19" x 33"

A matching pair of sawhorses—made with loving care.

The legs and braces are notched for looks and rigidity.

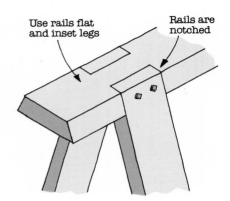

Use rails flat and inset legs

Rails are notched

Sawhorses – not all are made for sawing

Take the name literally and you use them only as racks on which you place wood for sawing. Call them multipurpose and they are supports for plant displays, workbenches, dining tables, even scaffolds. We've seen them knocked together quickly with scrap wood, and also made lovingly with hardwood and fancy joints. How you make them is a personal thing but—prideful projects or quickies put together with store-bought brackets—they are garden-functional! House builders are concerned only with function and usually use construction-grade softwood for sawhorses. If you're a gardener you may want something prettier—kiln-dried, straight-grain fir is stiff and looks good, or you may opt for maple, birch, or mahogany.

The key construction word is "rigid." A cross rail with legs lag-bolted on is sturdy but will hold up longer if you add a gusset or a brace. Legs set in notches are stronger because the insetting provides an antitwist action. Use a 2x6 placed flat to make it easier to cut the notches; you will also have a broader work surface.

Add a shelf to increase rigidity and provide a place to hold tools and fasteners. A plain shelf nailed to braces does the job, but a lipped one—shown with the "working horse" on page 51—will prevent materials from dropping off even when you carry the sawhorse.

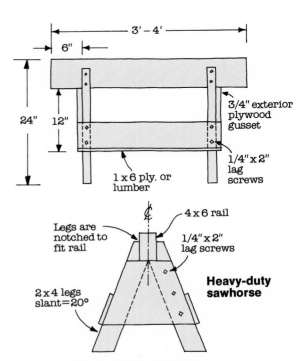

3' – 4'

6"

24"

12"

3/4" exterior plywood gusset

1/4" x 2" lag screws

1 x 6 ply. or lumber

Legs are notched to fit rail

4 x 6 rail

1/4" x 2" lag screws

2 x 4 legs slant = 20°

Heavy-duty sawhorse

– Use waterproof glue all joints
– Use washers under all lag screws

The matching sawhorses and a finished plywood top convert into a serving table.

Two matching horses and a duckboard top form a plant display platform.

Built to a lower height the sawhorses and plywood top serve as an outdoor dining table.

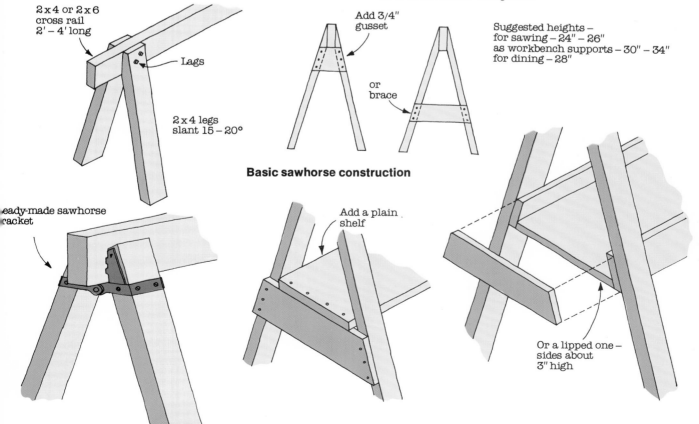

2 x 4 or 2 x 6
cross rail
2' – 4' long

Lags

2 x 4 legs
slant 15 – 20°

Add 3/4"
gusset

or
brace

Suggested heights –
for sawing – 24" – 26"
as workbench supports – 30" – 34"
for dining – 28"

Basic sawhorse construction

Ready-made sawhorse
bracket

Add a plain
shelf

Or a lipped one –
sides about
3" high

This combination storage box and sawhorse took on new dimensions when we added wheels.

The Roll-Around Sawhorse

If you want a very practical, platform-type, storage-box sawhorse, make this one but don't let anyone see it. Once on view, it will be appropriated for so many chores you will be forced to put wheels on it—and that will be followed closely by the children's request for a wooden horse's head mounted on the front. Maybe you should consider making a few!

Build the box first, using waterproof glue and 7d nails at all contact points. Attach the sides to the ends and then cut the bottom to exact size by measuring directly on assembly. Check detail "A" before you cut the plywood cover. The project will look better if you frame the plywood as shown. Also, solid lumber provides a more secure attachment for the hinge screws.

Saw carefully when you cut the slope angle on the legs—do one and use it as a pattern to mark the others. Attach the legs and then place the brace across them so you can mark the length and the angles required. Follow the same procedure to find the exact length of the shelf.

Detail "B" shows how to install the wheels. All are

The carpenter uses it for woodworking tools.

stock parts you can find in any handyman's center. Use a hacksaw to cut the axle after you have tested on assembly to determine the correct length. Don't forget the washers. These are needed to keep the wheels from rubbing against the sawhorse legs. The axle caps lock in place when you tap them home with a hammer.

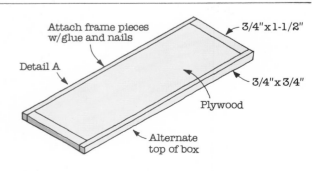

Attach frame pieces w/glue and nails

Detail A

3/4"x1-1/2"

3/4"x3/4"

Plywood

Alternate top of box

The home entertainer uses it for barbecue accessories.

The gardener uses it for garden equipment.

The kindergarten teacher uses it for toys.

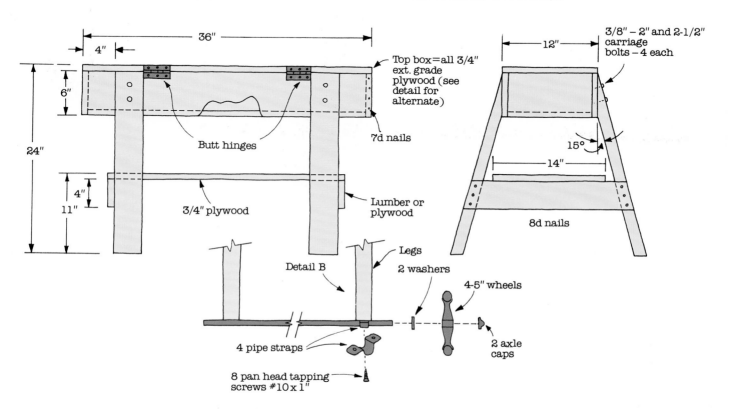

36"

4"

6"

24"

4"

11"

Butt hinges

3/4" plywood

Top box=all 3/4" ext. grade plywood (see detail for alternate)

7d nails

Lumber or plywood

12"

3/8" – 2" and 2-1/2" carriage bolts – 4 each

15°

14"

8d nails

Detail B

Legs

2 washers

4-5" wheels

4 pipe straps

2 axle caps

8 pan head tapping screws #10 x 1"

The hinged horses are sturdy. We have put as much as 200 pounds on each with no problem.

The Hinged Horse

These light-duty, folding sawhorses, called "Tennessee Walkers" by our man in Los Angeles, store neatly on a fence until needed for a sawing chore or supports for a potting table or plant display.

It should take less than an evening to make a set—all you need for each horse is five pieces of 2 x 4 and a pair of hinges.

It will be easier to cut the legs accurately if you place four pieces of 2 x 4 edge-to-edge and make the 20-degree cuts across them instead of sawing them individually.

Attach the hinges to the top end of each leg, and then place them in position on the rail so you can drive the screws that secure the second hinge leaf.

They are easy to carry . . .

. . . and easy to store

Each horse
requires –
1 rail –
2" x 4" x 36"
4 legs – 2" x 4"
x 29" w/20°
cut at each end
2 pair – 3" hinges

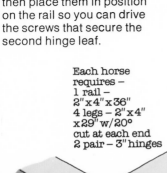

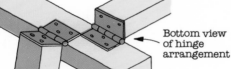

Bottom view
of hinge
arrangement

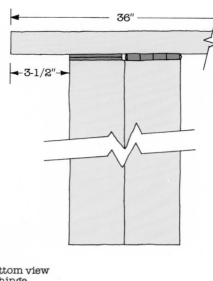

36"

3-1/2"

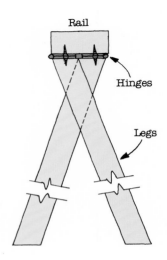

Rail

Hinges

Legs

A practical horse for garden woodwork has shelf for tools.

Garden Working Horse

This sawhorse is designed to take abuse and be practical for garden woodworking chores. The low height is good for sawing, the lipped shelf holds tools, and the unit is light enough to tote.

Form the legs first, sawing the slant cut on one and then using it as a pattern for the others. Attach the legs to the rail with lags but be sure to use the lengths specified and to stagger them as shown in the drawing.

Cut the sides and ends of the tray by measuring for correct length on the assembly. Attach the sides first, by nailing into the legs from the inside, and then add the ends. Bevel the long edges of the bottom piece to match the angle of the sides.

Skip this if you wish because square edges on the bottom will not be visible inside the tray (see detail).

The optional 2 x 6 cap will increase the working surface of the sawhorse. If you add it, use 16d nails to attach it to the rail.

Its low height is good for hand sawing.

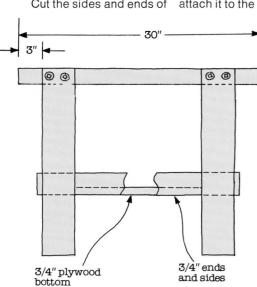

30"

3"

3/4" plywood bottom

3/4" ends and sides

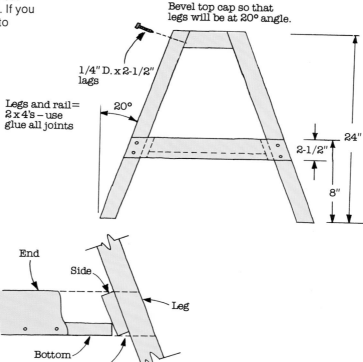

Bevel top cap so that legs will be at 20° angle.

1/4" D. x 2-1/2" lags

Legs and rail = 2 x 4's – use glue all joints

20°

24"

2-1/2"

8"

End

Side

Leg

Bottom

No bevel method

Tables and their supports

Table structures should be uncomplicated, strong, and durable. You can take some liberties with the dimensions of end tables and coffee tables, but not with tables designed for dining. This is one project area where function definitely dictates proportions.

Table height must permit comfortable seating—table size must allow elbow room for each person. Minimum width for a square table for four is 32 inches, but 36 inches is better. If the table is round, provide a 36-inch diameter for four people, 48 inches for six. A rectangular table for eight should measure about 36 x 82 inches. A good general rule is to provide about 24 inches for each person.

The basic frames shown below can be used for any round, square, or rectangular table. Size the frame so overall dimensions are 4 inches less than the dimensions of the top.

Top slabs can be solid wood, plywood, plywood used as a core for another material, or special materials like wide-panel, edge-glued redwood. The latter is available in widths up to 36 inches, lengths up to 22 feet, and thicknesses from ¾ inch to 2 inches. It's especially good for table tops and other garden projects since the boards are bonded with a weatherproof resin.

The details on the next page show how to assemble various table tops. Solid boards can be butted or spaced. They can be nailed directly to the frame or preassembled with cleats and then secured with corner irons. Corner irons can also be used for plywood tops, whether used alone or as a core for other materials.

The basic table pedestal gives good support to . . .

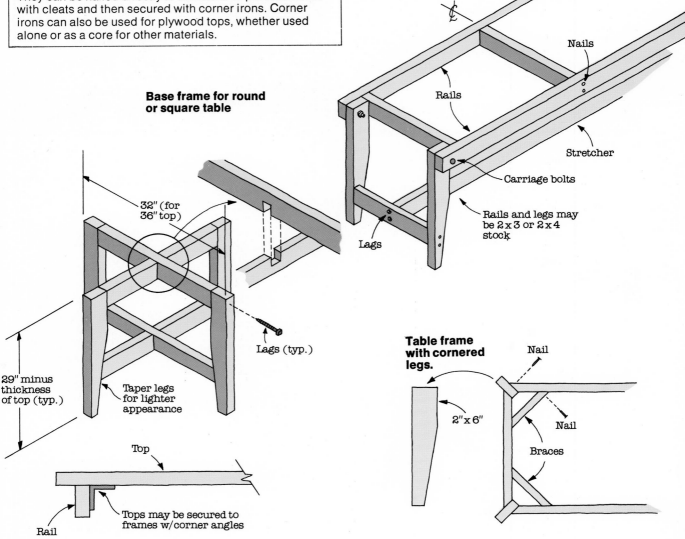

Base frame for square or rectangular table

Nails

Rails

Stretcher

Carriage bolts

Lags

Rails and legs may be 2 x 3 or 2 x 4 stock

Base frame for round or square table

32" (for 36" top)

Lags (typ.)

29" minus thickness of top (typ.)

Taper legs for lighter appearance

Top

Rail

Tops may be secured to frames w/corner angles

Table frame with cornered legs.

Nail

2" x 6"

Nail

Braces

. . . a removable square top . . .   *. . . or round top*

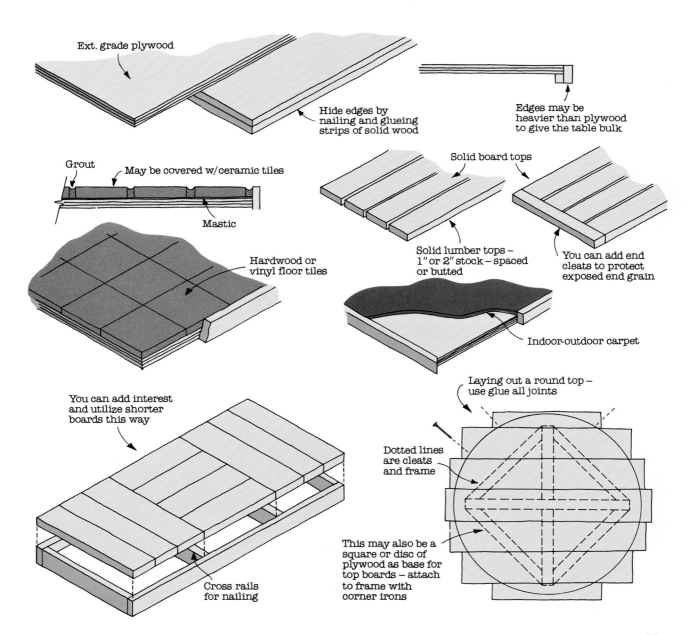

Ext. grade plywood

Hide edges by nailing and glueing strips of solid wood

Edges may be heavier than plywood to give the table bulk

Grout

May be covered w/ceramic tiles

Mastic

Solid board tops

Hardwood or vinyl floor tiles

Solid lumber tops – 1" or 2" stock – spaced or butted

You can add end cleats to protect exposed end grain

Indoor-outdoor carpet

You can add interest and utilize shorter boards this way

Cross rails for nailing

Laying out a round top – use glue all joints

Dotted lines are cleats and frame

This may also be a square or disc of plywood as base for top boards – attach to frame with corner irons

Rugged top has cut-out for plastic container "sink." Garden hose is hooked to simple plumbing for running water.

Vegetable clean-up table

Here's a special table where you can top vegetables and remove soil before bringing them into the kitchen. Ours includes a cutout for a rigid plastic container (or a sink) and some simple plumbing you can connect to a garden hose. You can omit this feature, if you wish, and just put a container of water directly on the table.

Cut legs and top rails to length and assemble with lags as shown in the detail. Drill 1-inch holes about ¾ inch deep, then center-drill for the lags. Glue the dowel plugs in place after the lags are tightened.

Cut and install the shelf rails, and then add the boards. We call for finishing nails you can set and hide, but work with common or box nails if you prefer.

Cut the top boards and make the cutout for the sink. Install the cross rails so they will provide support on each side of the cutout. Secure the boards with 12d or 16d nails.

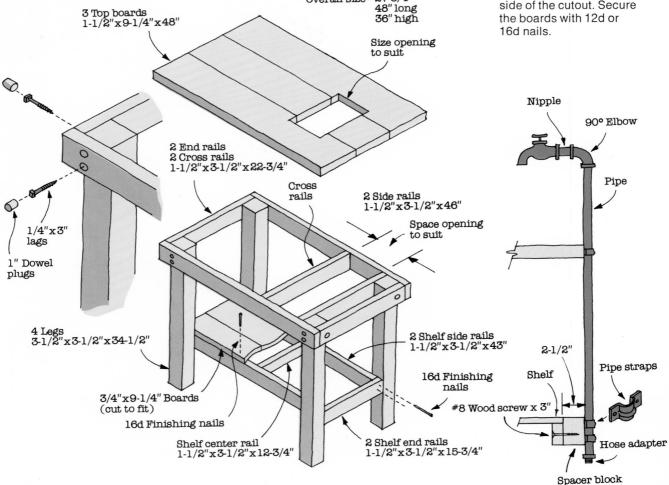

Overall size=27-3/4"
48" long
36" high

3 Top boards
1-1/2"x9-1/4"x48"

Size opening to suit

2 End rails
2 Cross rails
1-1/2"x3-1/2"x22-3/4"

Cross rails

2 Side rails
1-1/2"x3-1/2"x46"

Space opening to suit

1/4"x3" lags

1" Dowel plugs

4 Legs
3-1/2"x3-1/2"x34-1/2"

3/4"x9-1/4" Boards
(cut to fit)

16d Finishing nails

Shelf center rail
1-1/2"x3-1/2"x12-3/4"

2 Shelf side rails
1-1/2"x3-1/2"x43"

16d Finishing nails

#8 Wood screw x 3"

2 Shelf end rails
1-1/2"x3-1/2"x15-3/4"

Nipple

90° Elbow

Pipe

2-1/2"

Shelf

Pipe straps

#8 Wood screw x 3"

Hose adapter

Spacer block

The low table is used as a coffee table or end table.

Low Table with Butcher-Block Top

The living room has its end tables; our garden has low tables like this one, with built-in handholes so you can tote them easily. The project really came about because of a number of 2x4 cutoffs we regarded as a challenge instead of a waste.

If you own a few bar clamps, you can assemble the slab with glue only, maintaining clamp pressure until the glue is dry. Do the job *without* clamps by following the glue-and-nail procedure shown in the detail.

Cut sides to length and place them against the slab so you can mark nail locations. Drill a ⅜-inch hole, ¼ inch deep at each mark and then, after coating contact points with glue, attach the sides by nailing through the holes. Use a nail set to sink the nails. Add the legs by nailing into the slab—the ends by driving lag bolts.

Coat all nail holes with glue and tap in dowels that are a bit longer than necessary. Sand them flush when the glue dries.

Projects like this deserve a smooth finish. We suggest a thorough sanding followed by a generous application of sealer. Let the sealer soak in for about 30 minutes and then wipe off any excess with a lint-free cloth. Sand lightly again in about 24 hours. Repeat the sealer-sanding procedure in a month or so.

Hand holes are built in so table can be moved easily.

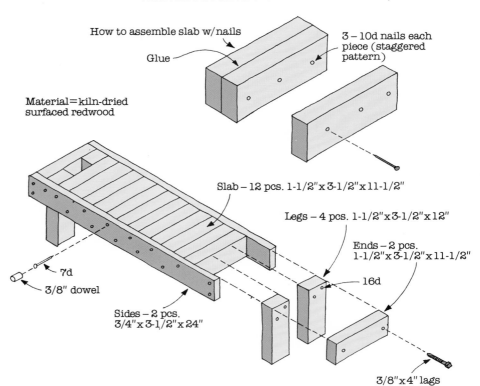

How to assemble slab w/nails

Glue

3 – 10d nails each piece (staggered pattern)

Material=kiln-dried surfaced redwood

Slab – 12 pcs. 1-1/2"x3-1/2"x11-1/2"

Legs – 4 pcs. 1-1/2"x3-1/2"x12"

Ends – 2 pcs. 1-1/2"x3-1/2"x11-1/2"

16d

7d

3/8" dowel

Sides – 2 pcs. 3/4"x3-1/2"x24"

3/8"x4" lags

Playing checkers on a field of Scotch and Irish moss.

With sturdy legs and wheels the table moves easily.

Pan's Checkerboard Table

If the god of fields, forests, and flocks had a yen for checkers or chess, he would certainly want to play on a table like this. The project takes a little doing but it will always be a conversation piece.

Start construction by assembling the frame. Cut the miters carefully. Set all finishing nails so you can conceal them later with a wood dough. To be sure the bottom fits exactly, use the frame as a pattern. Cut four legs to length and attach them at the corners of the bottom with the lag screws called for. Cut the braces to exact length by measuring right on the assembly. Note: the top ends of the braces are secured by nailing through the bottom, but the opposite end is toe-nailed into the leg. Now you can attach the understructure to the frame by nailing from the outside

into the edges of the bottom. Run a bead of caulking inside, completely around the frame-to-bottom joint. This is so water will escape only where you provide drain holes.

Check the drawing detail for the procedure to follow when doing the egg-crate that provides the squares. If you have a table saw, you can use a dado assembly to cut the notches. With a handsaw, you can still stack the pieces to make outline saw cuts, but then separate them and work with a chisel to remove the waste. Assemble the pieces as shown, using only glue at each crossing.

Put a layer of potting

soil in the frame so the top of the egg-crate will be flush with the top edges of the frame. Drive a few 6d finishing nails through the frame and into selected partitions of the egg-crate. This is not to add strength, but to prevent the egg-crate from sinking.

The squares are filled alternately with Scotch moss (light green) and Irish moss (dark green). Buy the moss in flats and cut pieces so they fill the squares. Start with Scotch

moss in the first left-hand corner.

As for the 24 checkers you need, you have a choice. Buy readymade ones—they *do* come in large sizes. Or, use a 2-inch or 2½-inch hole saw in a drill press or portable drill to cut disks from ¼-inch or ½-inch stock; or cut ½-inch-thick pieces from a length of closet pole.

Stain 12 checkers one color and 12 another color or natural finish.

See detail for egg crate construction

Frame – 4 pcs. 1-1/2" x 5-1/2" x 27-1/2"

45° miter all corners

10d finishing nails into bottom

6d finishing nails (typ.)

Bottom – 1 pc. 3/4" ext. gr. plywood 24-1/2" sq.

Drain holes

Stack egg crate pieces, then notch

2-5/8"

1/2"

Use glue all crossings

14 pcs. 1/2" x 4" x 24-1/2"

2"

Optional stem for plate type casters

Toenail 8d

8d

3/8" x 2-1/2" lag w/ washer on each leg

Legs – 4 pcs. 3-1/2" x 3-1/2" x 17-1/2"

5"

Braces – 8 pcs. 1-1/2" x 3-1/2" cut to length on assembly

Every good gardener can use a potting table.

Potting table

The height of the potting table should suit the user. Consider how tall you are and how you like to work—standing or sitting—and the height of pots. Check by standing in front of a dining table, a kitchen counter, a workbench; one may be right for you. If not, design accordingly. The height you need may not be average, but this is *your* project.

First, attach the top boards to the cleats, then cut the legs to provide the height you decided on. Join the legs at the crossing point and secure them to the top. Note that one leg is fastened to the top and its mate is secured to the cleat. Cut the braces to fit and attach them as shown.

The height of the table should fit the worker most comfortably.

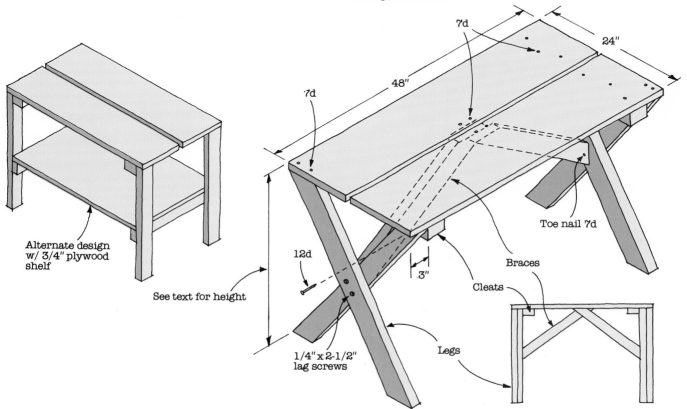

Alternate design
w/ 3/4" plywood
shelf

See text for height

7d

7d

24"

48"

12d

3"

1/4" x 2-1/2"
lag screws

Toe nail 7d

Braces

Cleats

Legs

A lovely garden, a simple bench and our favorite people—all were made for each other. H-legs are used to support the bench top.

Garden benches

Benches provide seating anywhere in the garden—on a patio, under a tree, even grouped as a conversation pit in sun or shade. One bench is never enough, so production is in order, whether you make several similar ones or provide more eye appeal by varying the designs.

Bench heights are limited so they will be comfortable for the average person, but widths and lengths can vary so long as the understructure provides good support. Tops can be boards or plywood, or they can be cut from a panel of edge-glued redwood. Use rails between supports when the top is plywood or a similar material—stretchers make sense no matter what the material or design since they contribute rigidity and durability.

X-legs are a popular design and can be done with a lap joint at the crossing point or by using a spacer and the rail *between* the legs, as shown in the detail below. Both ideas will work, but the lap crossing is the stronger of the two.

You can provide storage space in a plywood-top bench by following the suggestions on the next page. Half-inch plywood is adequate for the bottom. A continuous hinge may be substituted for the 3 or 4 butt hinges called for in the drawing.

All the base designs, except for the one marked "A," can be made with 2 x 3 or 2 x 4 material. The exception calls for two pieces of 2 x 8 or 2 x 10 stock with edges shaped as shown and with a notch to receive a stretcher. Project will have a heavy, hand-hewn look if you rough up edges with a rasp and use 2 x 8 or 2 x 10 stock for top.

Bench widths available w/standard boards

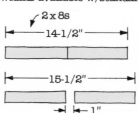

2 x 6's — 11" / 12" / 1"

2 x 8s — 14-1/2" / 15-1/2" / 1"

2 x 10s — 18-1/2" / 19-1/2" / 1"

Bench length and overhang for 2" x " material

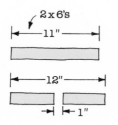
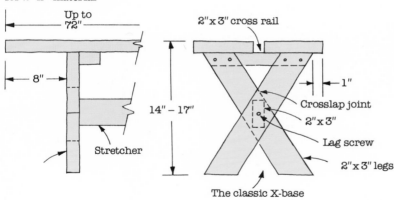
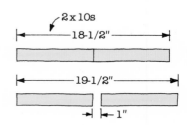
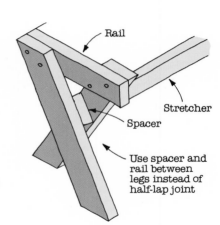

Up to 72"

8"

Stretcher

2" x 3" cross rail

14" – 17"

1"

Crosslap joint

2" x 3"

Lag screw

2" x 3" legs

The classic X-base

Rail

Stretcher

Spacer

Use spacer and rail between legs instead of half-lap joint

Above: Basic bench with X-legs. Right: Instant bench—a 4 x 12 timber resting on 10 x 10 legs. Looks permanent but is portable.

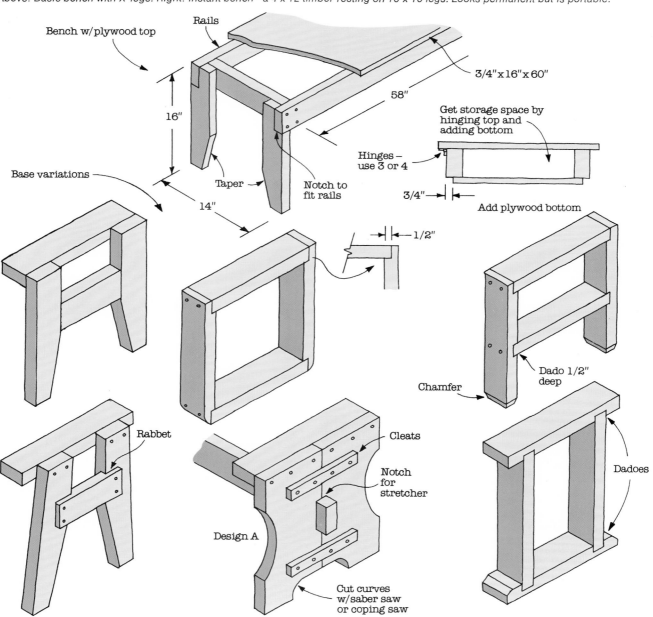

Bench w/plywood top

Rails

3/4"x16"x60"

58"

16"

14"

Taper

Notch to fit rails

Get storage space by hinging top and adding bottom

Hinges – use 3 or 4

3/4"

Add plywood bottom

Base variations

1/2"

Dado 1/2" deep

Chamfer

Rabbet

Cleats

Notch for stretcher

Design A

Dadoes

Cut curves w/saber saw or coping saw

Benches around the "campfire"—ready for a songfest or wienie roast.

Stack all four benches for a patio bar.

Firepit Benches

These unique benches can be used individually or as modules forming a table cover for a firepit. Separate them and they provide campfire seating; stack them and they serve as a higher table or as a bar. Our project includes two open and two closed benches that will span firepits up to 30 inches in diameter.

Work with a good grade of kiln-dried or air-dried lumber. You must cut the slots carefully, so make a cardboard pattern to mark the cut areas on each piece. Size the slots so parts will slip together without being forced. Forcing can create stresses which will eventually cause splitting or cracking.

Do not use glue or nails when joining legs to legs, or legs to closers. Secure the

Benches moved together to form table cover over firepit.

Stack two benches for a small picnic table.

tops by driving 12d or 16d nails—two into each leg; two or three between legs if closers are used. Drill pilot holes for the nails that secure the legs.

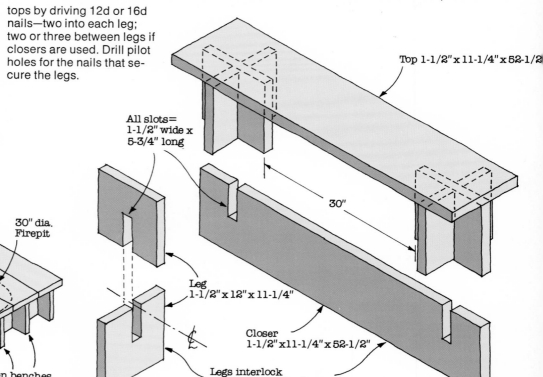

Top 1-1/2" x 11-1/4" x 52-1/2"

All slots = 1-1/2" wide x 5-3/4" long

30"

Leg 1-1/2" x 12" x 11-1/4"

Closer 1-1/2" x 11-1/4" x 52-1/2"

Legs interlock together or with closer

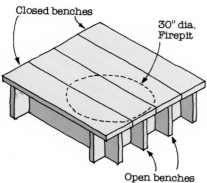

Closed benches

30" dia. Firepit

Open benches

The bench is heavy but portable enough for two people to move.

It looks at home on deck, patio or lawn.

Deck-top Bench

This bench will look at home on grass, concrete, or a wooden deck. It's sturdy, yet portable enough if two people choose to move it. Like a deck or duckboard the slab pieces are spaced for quick drainage and easy cleaning.

Cut all slab pieces to length. Mark the dowel locations on one piece and drill a small pilot hole at each point. Use this as a pattern, drilling through the pilot holes into each of the other pieces. Enlarge the holes to 1¼ inches. Start assembling the slab by inserting the dowels in one piece and driving nails through the bottom edge, as shown in the drawing detail. Keep adding pieces, nailing in similar fashion, using a piece of ¼ -inch plywood as a spacer. It isn't necessary to cut the dowels to exact length right off. If they are oversize, you can trim them after all slab pieces are assembled.

Put the legs and rails together as separate sections. Two carriage bolts through each leg may seem a bit much, but they will prevent the pivot action that can occur if you use just one.

Place the slab bottom-up and set the leg assemblies in position. Mark locations for the lag screws so they

will hit the center of slab pieces. Drill 5/16-inch holes through the rails, 3/16-inch holes part way into the slab pieces. Do not use glue when you attach the leg assemblies—you might want to remove them sometime so the slab can be set on taller supports and used as a table.

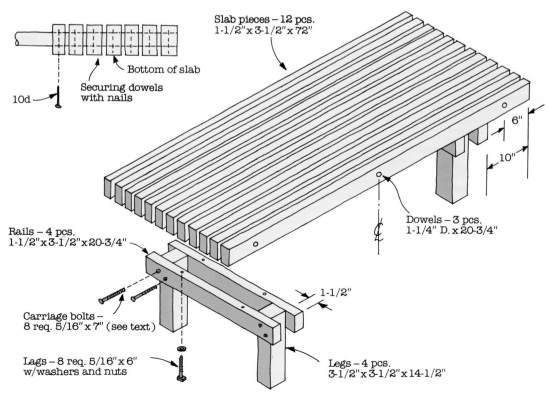

Rope and wood combine with coleus for a rustic combination.

Sky gardens

We asked ourselves, "Why must the hanging garden be a wire basket or a ceramic pot?," and answered the question with the five projects shown here. Wood may not be as flexible as wire or clay but its shapes can be as infinite as your imagination. With a lathe, you can even do the usual bowl or dome form. Wood, however, does not have to imitate anything—its own character is a prime feature of the project.

Our designs offer a visual change of pace. Choose the ones that best suit your plants. Some are quickies, others require more attention to detail, but all of them will contribute to the special appeal of the eye-level garden.

The boxes may be hung with cord or wire but we find a light chain very appropriate. Types available in small sizes include single jack, passing link, twist link, and straight link. Use screw eyes in the box, screw hooks as the hanger.

Dowel and chain suspend this column of cascading alyssum.

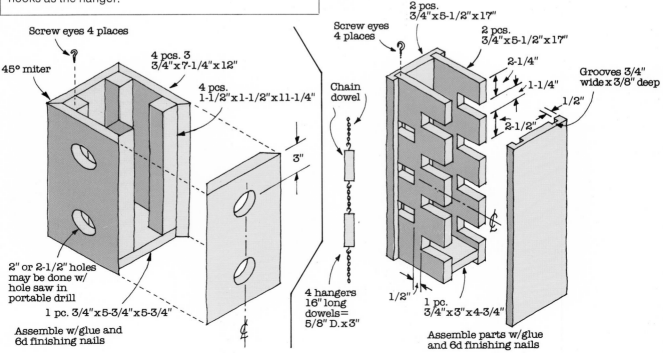

Screw eyes 4 places

45° miter

4 pcs. 3
3/4"x7-1/4"x12"

4 pcs.
1-1/2"x1-1/2"x11-1/4"

3"

2" or 2-1/2" holes
may be done w/
hole saw in
portable drill

1 pc. 3/4"x5-3/4"x5-3/4"

Assemble w/glue and
6d finishing nails

Chain
dowel

4 hangers
16" long
dowels=
5/8" D.x3"

Screw eyes
4 places

2 pcs.
3/4"x5-1/2"x17"

2 pcs.
3/4"x5-1/2"x17"

2-1/4"

1-1/4"

2-1/2"

1/2"

Grooves 3/4"
wide x 3/8" deep

1/2"

1 pc.
3/4"x3"x4-3/4"

Assemble parts w/glue
and 6d finishing nails

Eye level view of plants and wood creates a mood of its own.

This hanging wood potholder is a simple yet rewarding project.

Building blocks of redwood provide a simple, inexpensive means of housing a plant.

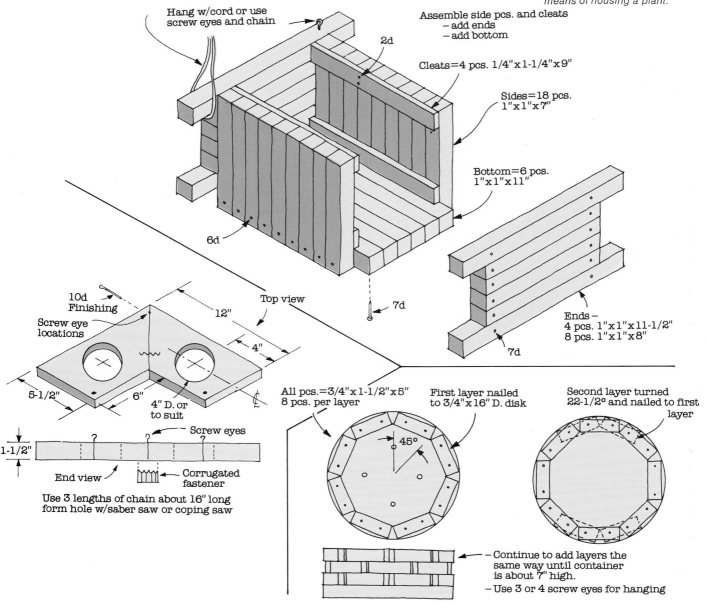

Hang w/cord or use screw eyes and chain

2d

Assemble side pcs. and cleats
— add ends
— add bottom

Cleats=4 pcs. 1/4"x1-1/4"x9"

Sides=18 pcs. 1"x1"x7"

Bottom=6 pcs. 1"x1"x11"

6d

7d

Ends –
4 pcs. 1"x1"x11-1/2"
8 pcs. 1"x1"x8"

7d

10d Finishing

Screw eye locations

Top view

12"

4"

5-1/2"

6"

4" D. or to suit

1-1/2"

Screw eyes

End view

Corrugated fastener

Use 3 lengths of chain about 16" long form hole w/saber saw or coping saw

All pcs.=3/4"x1-1/2"x5"
8 pcs. per layer

First layer nailed to 3/4"x16" D. disk

45°

Second layer turned 22-1/2° and nailed to first layer

– Continue to add layers the same way until container is about 7" high.
– Use 3 or 4 screw eyes for hanging

A-frame design provides a pyramid of color where you want it.

Pot displays

Plants in pots can be as changeable as the gardener wishes, whether for different color or display of seasonal favorites. Maybe the pots aren't works of art; but if you stage the right setting for them, even the prosaic clay pot acquires stature and shows its contents proudly.

The shelves you make for pot displays let you place a garden anywhere—on a fence or wall, under a window for viewing from either side of the glass, on a concrete patio to destroy the parking-lot look, on lawns and even driveways.

The project is sturdy, but light enough to carry where needed.

A-frame pot shelves

Make the legs first by following the detail in the drawing—shaping one part and then using it as a pattern for the others. An alternate method, which may prove more accurate, is to cut two leg pieces a few inches longer than necessary and then saw the sharp angle at the top end of each. Mate the two pieces and then use a straight board across the bottom to mark the base angle. All other parts, except the top shelf support, may be cut to the sizes called out in the drawing.

Hold the legs together by driving one or two small nails at the top. Place them in position on the bottom 2x4 and drill through for the ¼-inch carriage bolts. Secure the bolts and then follow the same drilling procedure for the top shelf support.

Add the shelves to complete the project. You can extend the length of this project by making a third leg assembly and adding shelf support pieces to the outside surface of one of the legs already put together (see drawing). Here, use 5-inch carriage bolts so you can pass through both shelf supports and the leg.

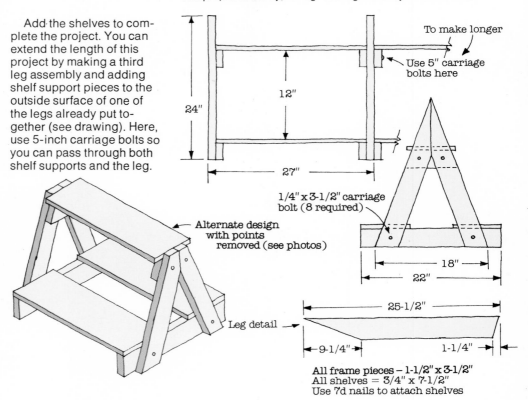

To make longer
Use 5" carriage bolts here

24"
12"
27"

1/4" x 3-1/2" carriage bolt (8 required)

Alternate design with points removed (see photos)

18"
22"

Leg detail

25-1/2"
9-1/4"
1-1/4"

All frame pieces – 1-1/2" x 3-1/2"
All shelves = 3/4" x 7-1/2"
Use 7d nails to attach shelves

The pot tree above is portable. It can be a permanent fixture by anchoring the 4x4 post in the ground.

Pot tree

Visualize the project as a complete assembly that you install in the ground. Select a straight, kiln-dried, S4S post for this project—an ordinary fence post won't do. Place the post across sawhorses or on a workbench. Chamfer the top end by working with a rasp or with a plane or by sawing, then mark the locations of the cross arms. Notches aren't difficult to do if you follow the instructions on page 91, but you can surface-mount them if you wish as shown in the detail drawing. In any event, use Douglas fir for the cross arms. Ask for 1x2 material and you will get the ¾-inch by 1½-inch stock called for in the sketch.

Attach the cross arms by using one of the methods shown and then shape the number of shelves you need, using one of the suggestions shown here or designing your own. Attach the shelves with glue and two or three nails into each support.

Set the project in the ground by following the procedure in the section on RAISED BEDS.

You can make the pot tree portable by adding the base shown in the photo above.

Design shelves to suit

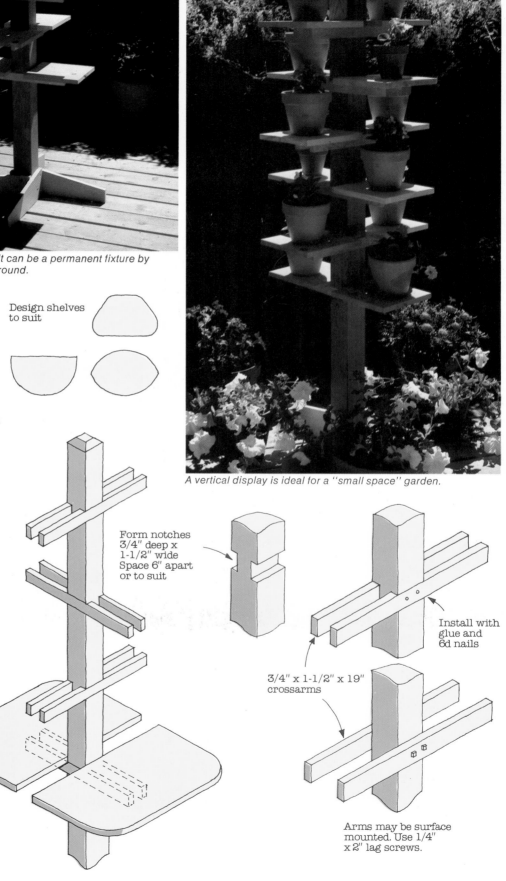

A vertical display is ideal for a "small space" garden.

Form notches
¾" deep x
1-1/2" wide
Space 6" apart
or to suit

Install with glue and 6d nails

¾" x 1-1/2" x 19" crossarms

Arms may be surface mounted. Use 1/4" x 2" lag screws.

A series of shelves turns a fence into a vertical garden.

A small shelf that is very sturdy.

Pot shelves

Any one of the three pot shelves detailed here can be built in an evening. Plot curves with a compass, or use a suitable pot lid or even a paint can as a pattern. When two brackets are required, form one and use it as a template to mark the other.

Use kiln-dried stock and apply a sealer after assembly. Redwood, knotty pine and fir are pretty enough if left natural but you can use a stain, as we did, if you wish.

Color stain was applied to blend shelves with fence.

Roughened edges give antique look.

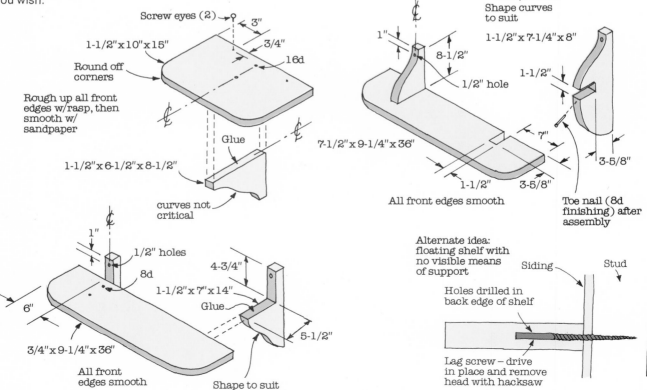

Screw eyes (2)
3"
1-1/2"x10"x15"
3/4"
Round off corners
16d
Rough up all front edges w/rasp, then smooth w/ sandpaper
Glue
1-1/2"x6-1/2"x8-1/2"
curves not critical

Shape curves to suit
1"
8-1/2"
1/2" hole
1-1/2"x7-1/4"x8"
1-1/2"
7-1/2"x9-1/4"x36"
7"
3-5/8"
1-1/2"
3-5/8"
All front edges smooth
Toe nail (8d finishing) after assembly

1"
1/2" holes
8d
6"
4-3/4"
1-1/2"x7"x14"
Glue
5-1/2"
3/4"x9-1/4"x36"
Shape to suit
All front edges smooth

Alternate idea: floating shelf with no visible means of support
Siding
Stud
Holes drilled in back edge of shelf
Lag screw – drive in place and remove head with hacksaw

The four pots in this display are all the weight this shelf will hold.

This single pot version is lightweight.

Quickie shelves

Quickie shelves—the kind of project that rewards way out of proportion to the construction time and material involved. Chances are you can cull the wood from leftovers.

The procedure for each project is the same. Assemble the sides to the front, then add the back. Cut the bottom pieces so they fit exactly. Nail them in place with equal spaces between. Be sure the front and back bottom-boards are nailed into the front and back pieces as well as into the sides.

The screw eyes and the chain shown in one drawing are optional. You can add them at some future date, should the shelf sag from the weight of the pots and exposure to weather.

To keep shelf from sagging, add chain shown in drawing.

Leftover wood scraps were used on this shelf.

Round corners
optional

Front – 1 pc.
3/4" x 2-1/2" x 36"

3 screw eyes

Back – 1 pc. 1-1/2" x 7-1/4" x 34-1/2"

4"

Cut off or
round off
corners

Back – 1 pc.
1-1/2" x 5-1/2" x 9"

Sides – 2 pcs.
3/4" x 2-1/2" x 8-1/4"

6d

2 1/2" holes or
2 screw eyes
for hanging

Bottom – 3 pcs.
3/4" x 2-1/2" x 7"

Front – 1 pc.
3/4" x 2-1/2" x 7"

8d (typ.)

Screw eyes
and chain
(optional)

6d

8d

Bottom – 2 pcs.
3/4" x 1-1/2" x 36"

Bottom – 2 pcs.
3/4" x 2-1/2" x 36"

8d (typ.)

Canvas version of the knee pad.

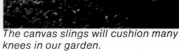

The canvas slings will cushion many knees in our garden.

Odds and ends

What is garden woodworking all about? It's using tools that beg to be used. It's answering the sawdust call. It's building wooden projects for living things to go in or around them—especially projects that can be done in a weekend. They can be practical, simply decorative, or fun things like a swing. The projects on the next 10 pages are some of our ideas. You will probably create many of your own.

Knee pads

Working close to the soil is one thing, but getting gardener's knee is something else. Here is a set of cushions for kneeling comfort.

Start the canvas version by attaching the supports to the base with glue and 8d nails. Use a file or rasp, followed by sandpaper, to round off the top edges of all three supports. This will break the sharp corners that might wear the canvas excessively. Attach the canvas to the center support first. Don't pull it taut across the span to the outer supports; allow it to sag about ½ inch.

Note that all canvas-attachment points involve the use of battens. These are necessary to keep the canvas from tearing away from the fasteners when you apply your weight.

The second version is just a thick pad with understrips that secure the indoor-outdoor carpet cover. You can use strips of double-faced carpeting tape to hold the foam rubber to the base, or you can work with either rubber cement or contact cement. Secure the cover along one side first. Then pull it across and nail down along the opposite side.

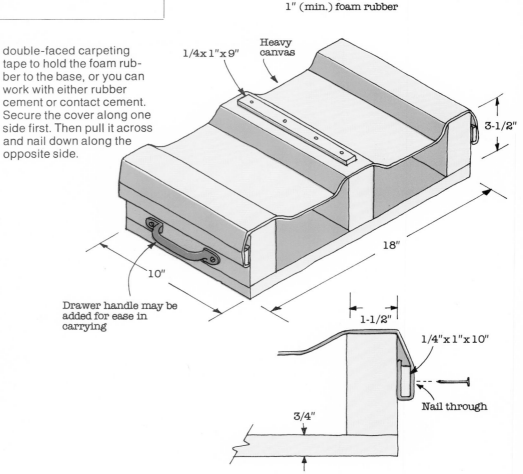

Alternate version: Indoor-outdoor carpet

3/4"x4"x10"   3/4"x10"x18"   4d nails
1" (min.) foam rubber

Heavy canvas
1/4x1"x9"
3-1/2"
18"
10"
Drawer handle may be added for ease in carrying
1-1/2"
1/4"x1"x10"
Nail through
3/4"

A small storage area was built into this gardenized version of the traditional five board stool.

Tote bench

Make it with a nail-down top for just sitting or standing on, or add a bottom and hinge the top to provide a compartment for pruning shears and such. Do the legs first by boring a 1 or 1½-inch hole and then making the two slanted saw cuts. Form the notches (see page 91) for the sides and then assemble with water-proof glue and nails or screws. Shape the finger slot in the top by boring two 1½-inch holes and then cutting between them with a compass or coping saw.

Inset the bottom, if you use one, and secure with glue and nails. The side detail shows the addition of a wood strip to provide more strength for the hinge screws.

Stand on it—for extra reach, but be sure it rests firmly on level ground.

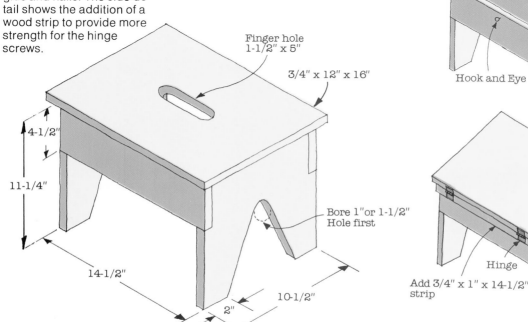

Sit on it—to do various chores more comfortably.

Light enough to tote where needed.

Finger hole
1-1/2" x 5"

3/4" x 12" x 16"

4-1/2"

11-1/4"

Bore 1"or 1-1/2"
Hole first

14-1/2"

2"

10-1/2"

Hook and Eye

Hinge

Add 3/4" x 1" x 14-1/2"
strip

Add
Bottom

The center panel is peg-board for hanging tools.

The box is lightweight, small enough to "tote" around the garden.

Tote box

Start this project by cutting the base—a piece of ¾-inch exterior grade fir plywood 10½-inches by 22½-inches. Add the sides, then the two interior partitions. Make the two uprights and hold or clamp them together as you drill the hole for the handle. Cut four strips measuring ¾-inch by ¾-inch by 13-inches (or use ¾-inch, ¼ round molding) and attach them to the inside surfaces of the uprights as shown in the detail drawing. The space allowed between the strips should permit the perforated hardboard divider to fit loosely since it is a removable part.

Attach the uprights with screws, as shown, and then close in the box by adding the end pieces. Do not secure the handle since it should move out of place when you wish to remove the divider. If the dowel fits too snugly, reduce its diameter with sandpaper or enlarge the hole slightly with a file or rasp.

To use the project as a small greenhouse, just use a piece of dowel long enough to support the plastic cover.

Use the center space for nursery transplants—and end spaces for garden tools and seeds.

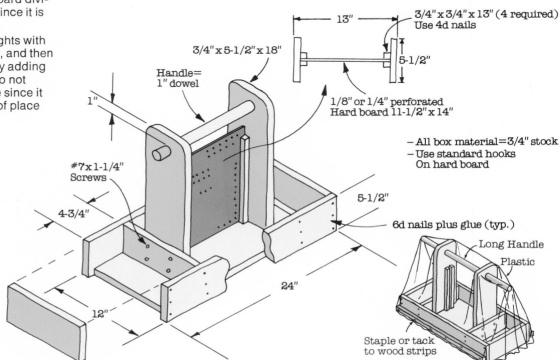

13"

3/4" x 3/4" x 13" (4 required)
Use 4d nails

3/4" x 5-1/2" x 18"

5-1/2"

Handle = 1" dowel

1/8" or 1/4" perforated
Hard board 11-1/2" x 14"

1"

— All box material = 3/4" stock
— Use standard hooks
  On hard board

#7 x 1-1/4" Screws

5-1/2"

4-3/4"

6d nails plus glue (typ.)

12"

24"

Long Handle

Plastic

Staple or tack
to wood strips

Wheels added to the tool box makes moving it a one-man job.

Adding a plastic top turns the box into a mini-greenhouse.

Multiuse carpenter's box

The gardener's carpenter box is large enough to hold a good assortment of tools. Mounted on casters, it is easily moved to any construction site.

Cut and assemble the sides, ends, and bottom—then add the divider and the partitions. The latter can be spaced evenly or adjusted to suit a particular requirement. Add the two outside stiffeners by nailing into ends and sides of the box; the center piece by nailing only into the sides.

Cut the handle supports to length and round off the top ends to eliminate sharp corners. Hold the two parts together while you form the hole for the handle. Before you attach the supports, cut the dowel-handle to length and insert it in the holes to act as an alignment guide when you drive the screws that secure the supports. Lock the handle in place by driving one 8d finishing nail down from the top of each support.

Use waterproof glue, in addition to the fasteners called for, in all joints. Attach the swivel-action, plate-type casters with #10 x ¾" panhead tapping screws.

Or you can use it as a movable flower bed.

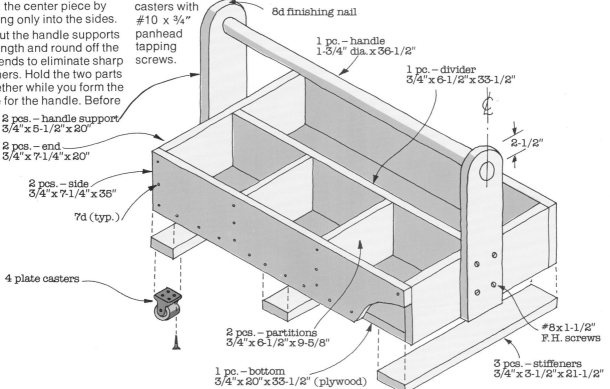

8d finishing nail

1 pc. – handle
1-3/4" dia. x 36-1/2"

1 pc. – divider
3/4" x 6-1/2" x 33-1/2"

2-1/2"

2 pcs. – handle support
3/4" x 5-1/2" x 20"

2 pcs. – end
3/4" x 7-1/4" x 20"

2 pcs. – side
3/4" x 7-1/4" x 35"

7d (typ.)

4 plate casters

2 pcs. – partitions
3/4" x 6-1/2" x 9-5/8"

1 pc. – bottom
3/4" x 20" x 33-1/2" (plywood)

#8 x 1-1/2"
F.H. screws

3 pcs. – stiffeners
3/4" x 3-1/2" x 21-1/2"

Three solid 3-legged stools built to stay in the family for generations to come.

3-legged stools

The classic picture of a milkmaid shows her carrying a 3-legged stool. We feel this time-honored stool is at home in the garden as well as the barn. Why a tripod? Probably because three legs are lighter than four and are more stable on uneven ground.

The key principles are low height and sturdiness, regardless of whether you do the basic round top with heavy dowel legs or a super version with curved feet and molded edges.

Round feet, except for the readymade variety that you attach with a metal plate, will be sturdy if you wedge-lock them as shown in the detail. Make the hole a snug fit for the leg—shape the wedge so it must be forced into the slot. Coat all contact points with glue before

assembling the pieces. Both the wedge and the leg should extend slightly above the seat so you can sand them flush after the glue dries.

Install curved legs with screws, then conceal the screws with wooden plugs. Here too, you should glue-coat all contact points before assembly. Wipe off excess glue immediately with a damp cloth.

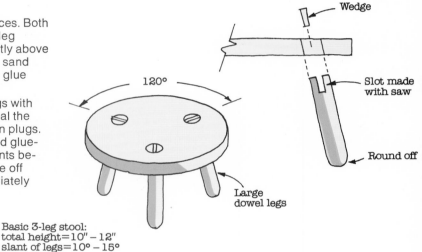

Basic 3-leg stool:
total height=10" – 12"
slant of legs=10° – 15°

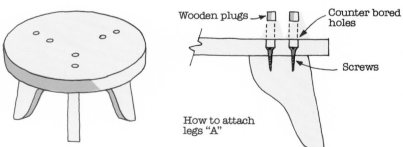

How to attach legs "A"

Try something different with fiddle back design

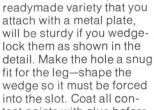

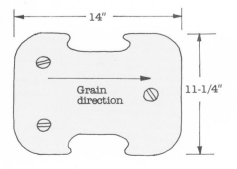

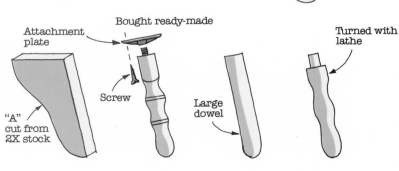

Legs to use

The dowel swing at rest.

The swing's cradle shape gives comfort to its passengers.

Dowel swing

Large dowel—often called "closet pole"—a scrap piece of hose, and some heavy nylon rope are all you need to construct the swing.

Cut dowels to length and then use a rasp and sandpaper to round off both ends of each piece. Drilling the holes accurately will not be a problem if you follow the suggestions shown in the detail. The longitudinal mark will provide a common centerline for the holes—the drilling jig will assure that all holes have the same edge distance. Use ½-inch or ¾-inch stock for the jig and size it so it fits the dowel snugly. Drill small pilot holes first. Be sure the dowels are held firmly when you enlarge the pilot holes to full size. Use sandpaper to smooth both ends of each hole.

Form the hole through the handgrips by drilling from both ends. Work slowly and carefully so the bit will not wander.

Spacers can be cut from some scrap garden hose with a sharp knife dipped frequently in water, or by using a fine-tooth saw.

Study the drawing carefully before you start assembly. Be sure to include knots at all indicated places.

Hand grips can be adjusted to another position for child's grip. A pillow adds extra comfort.

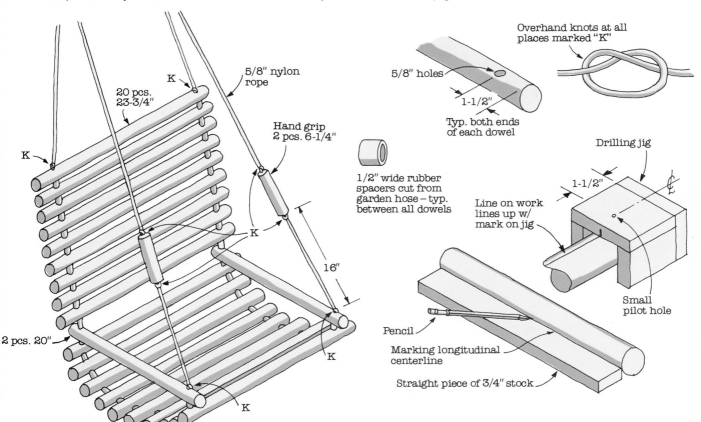

The story project measures 3-feet high by 5-feet deep by 9-feet long. Make it shorter if you wish but do not reduce the height. The front boards are removable so you can add or subtract to suit the height of the compost.

Compost bin

Compost is an excellent mulch and soil conditioner that you make at home by composting various kinds of non-woody plant refuse, such as grass clippings, leaves, plant tops from the vegetable and flower garden, etc. The partially decomposed material rates as one of the best organic mulches, although it may not be the most attractive.

The bin will hold generous amounts of compost and is designed to provide the air circulation so important for proper decomposition. View the job as four dividers which are held sturdily by the boards across the back and by the pipe reinforcement at the front.

All the materials, except the filler strips and the removable boards can be precut to the lengths called out

in the materials list. Start construction by joining parts B and C. Note the 2x4s of the inside dividers are centered on the 2x6s; those on the end dividers are attached along an edge.

Join these sub-assemblies by nailing on all of the boards, part D. Remember to leave the 1-inch space at the front (see detail in drawing). After you add the filler strips, you will have a groove for the removable boards to slide in. Last step on the dividers, before you attach parts A, is to nail on part E to cover the opening left by the two bottom boards.

Prepare the bin area, preferably in a sunny location, by leveling and tamping the ground. Space the dividers to provide the overall length you decide on and

then add the three back boards, part G.

When driving the pipes, hold them snugly against the front surface of the dividers. Keep them centered so they will stay vertical. Use a sledge to do the job but don't attempt to swing like a railroad worker. Settle for driving the pipe as far as you can if the ground is too hard for full 3-foot pene-

tration. Then use a hacksaw to cut the top end flush. Use a file to remove the burrs that remain. Add the pipe clamps but use large, panhead, sheet metal screws instead of conventional wood screws; they will hold better.

Apply any finish material, such as a water seal, before you staple the wire fabric in place.

Materials list

A = 4 pcs. 2″ x 6″ x 60″
B = 8 pcs. 2″ x 6″ x 34½″
C = 8 pcs. 2″ x 4″ x 34½″
D = 18 pcs. 1″ x 6″ x 54½″—use boards or
     cut from ext. grade plywood.
E = 2 pcs. 1″ x 3″ x 47½″
F = 1″ x 2″ stock cut length to suit
G = 3 pcs. 2″ x 6″ x 9′
H = Optional number of 1″ x 6″ boards or ext.
     grade plywood. Cut lengths to suit.
     4 pcs. ¾″ galvanized pipe, 6′ long
     12 pipe straps with screws
     About 45′ wire fabric

A board or two, placed across the top, provides a shelf for plant display. Attach a trellis if you wish. See TRELLIS section, page 22, for ideas.

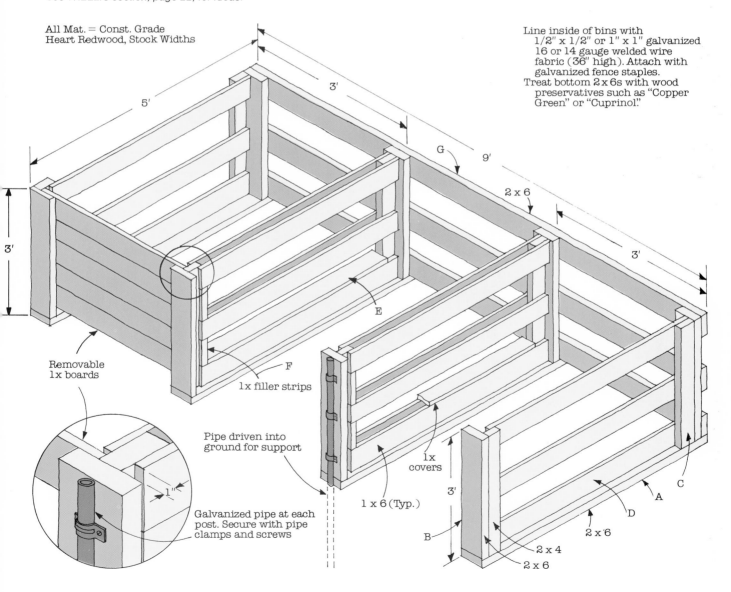

All Mat. = Const. Grade
Heart Redwood, Stock Widths

Line inside of bins with
1/2" x 1/2" or 1" x 1" galvanized
16 or 14 gauge welded wire
fabric (36" high). Attach with
galvanized fence staples.
Treat bottom 2 x 6s with wood
preservatives such as "Copper
Green" or "Cuprinol."

5'

3'

9'

2 x 6

3'

3'

G

E

F

Removable
1x boards

1x filler strips

1x
covers

1 x 6 (Typ.)

3'

Pipe driven into
ground for support

Galvanized pipe at each
post. Secure with pipe
clamps and screws

1"

B

2 x 4

2 x 6

2 x 6

A

D

C

The open box offers unrestricted use of the hose.

Hose box

What do you do with long lengths of hose you must have but are unsightly and a tripping hazard when left uncoiled? We made a pretty box with a hinged front and top so the hose will coil easily but be convenient to use.

Start construction by assembling the back and sides and then adding the bottom, the feet, and the compartment board. The latter forms the base of a triangle in one corner so ends must be cut at 45 degrees. Before installing, and before drilling the outlet hole for the hose, determine on which side of the faucet the box will be placed.

Make the drop-down front and the cover as separate assemblies, and then attach them to the box with hinges, surfaced-mounted as shown in the drawing.

You'll find it easier to coil the hose with the drop-front in closed position—drop the front when pulling the hose out. It's okay to keep the hose connected to the faucet but it's always wise to turn off the tap when the hose is not in use.

When closed, the hose out of sight and protected from the sun.

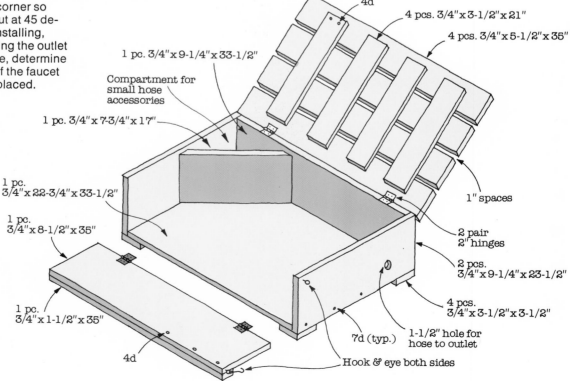

4d

4 pcs. 3/4" x 3-1/2" x 21"

4 pcs. 3/4" x 5-1/2" x 35"

1 pc. 3/4" x 9-1/4" x 33-1/2"

Compartment for small hose accessories

1 pc. 3/4" x 7-3/4" x 17"

1 pc. 3/4" x 22-3/4" x 33-1/2"

1 pc. 3/4" x 8-1/2" x 35"

1 pc. 3/4" x 1-1/2" x 35"

4d

1" spaces

2 pair 2" hinges

2 pcs. 3/4" x 9-1/4" x 23-1/2"

4 pcs. 3/4" x 3-1/2" x 3-1/2"

1-1/2" hole for hose to outlet

7d (typ.)

Hook & eye both sides

An edging can be bender board . . .　　　*. . . or a 1x6*　　　*. . . or 2x2's*

Keeping your garden shipshape

Edge a path, edge a border, edge a lawn with wood—and path, border, and lawn are under control. The wood may be a 1x6-inch board or short pieces of 4x4's set vertically in the ground. This is one use of wood that appeals to the orderly-minded garden-keeper. He's the captain of a tight ship. Everything's shipshape.

. . . or 2x4's　　　*. . . or 4x4's*

. . . or railroad ties　　　*. . . or logs or . . .*

Woodworker's talk

Tips on buying · The tools to use · Charts on nails, screws, bolts, and miscellaneous hardware · Techniques for sawing, drilling, and treating wood · A woodworker's illustrated glossary

Wood is workable, durable and beautiful. It's a natural material that responds graciously to love and care. An affinity with the material from ponderosa pine to Honduras mahogany, and a desire to do a commendable job are more important than whether you work with hand tools or power tools. A power saw is faster but many woodworkers claim a handsaw brings you closer to the true nature of the material with each cut made—and who's to argue?

An important factor is to consider a project as a reflection of yourself. A sloppy joint, regardless of whether it is a fancy one or a simple butt, does not say "bad wood," but "poor craftsmanship."

Woodworking has always been one of the world's most popular avocations. Who can enjoy it more than the gardener who is surrounded by wood in his work—wood growing, trees and shrubs, wood in a container or trellis, wood to sit on, stand on, wood to support a heavy espalier. What can blend more naturally in the garden?

Defects . . . so called

In our minds, there is no such thing as a bad piece of wood although there may be contortions that render a length of wood unusable, as is, for a particular application. For example, a 12-foot board in warp or wind (twist) usually will become usable if cut into shorter pieces that share a minimum amount of the total defect. "Flaws" which affect some people adversely, spark the opposite reaction in others.

Pecky cedar, the result of fungus activity on the heartwood of the tree

There is art in woodworking. The wood plane and shavings speak out in the "language" of the woodworker.

while it is growing, was once tolerated only in constructions where it could be hidden. Today it is often used on inside wall paneling. Knots, which are locations where a branch projected from the trunk, dark streaks, worm holes, are rejection factors to some, design details to others—especially in garden woodworking, where the formality of sleek inside furniture does not necessarily apply.

There are problem defects like *loose* knots, *checks,* which are splits usually occuring at the end of a board, and *pitch pockets,* which are large or small accumulations of resin that can occur anywhere and even in high grade, clear, kiln-dried stock.

One way to avoid these is simply to be persnickety when you buy, especially in the lower-grade lumber. Be like the shopper who, confronted with a bin of apples, walks away with a bagful convinced he has chosen the best. Most lumberyards catering to the homecraftperson have become serve-yourself places so there is no objection to being selective so long as you don't make a mess of the bin. You can also spend more money for higher grades of wood and so reduce the likelihood of problem defects.

Judgments should also be made in relation to the type of project. Patio tables and benches call for better grades of wood than do compost bins and header boards.

Softwoods and hardwoods

The terms must not be taken literally. It's not always possible to tell the difference by looking, or feeling, or even by sawing to determine denseness. The terms are botanical designations that tell basically whether the wood came from an evergreen or deciduous tree. There are exceptions. Some species of larch, tamarack and cypress, all softwoods, are not evergreen. Often, *softwood* applies to

conifers since all native softwood trees bear cones of one kind or another.

The point is that "hard" and "soft" are not descriptive of wood density or whether a particular species is easy or tough to saw. Some hardwood trees, like aspen and cottonwood, produce softer wood than softwood trees like white pine and the true firs. Some softwood trees, like Douglas fir and the longleaf pines produce wood as hard as the wood from hardwood trees like yellow poplar and basswood.

Cost and availability were our principal reasons for using soft woods rather than hard woods as project material. But, we also point out that the choice of wood we made for any project shown should not be accepted as bible. The builder's preference and the availability of materials in various areas of the country are also considerations. If we call for redwood or ponderosa pine or Douglas fir, it's your prerogative to use whatever wood you prefer or can find more easily or more cheaply.

The Softwood Grading Chart on the following page will define the differences between the many different grades you may find at the lumber yard.

Seasoning

Seasoning is a treatment that reduces the natural moisture content of green wood. Kiln-dried lumber has had its moisture content reduced to no more than 6% to 8% by placing it in special ovens where climate can be controlled. The process, at the start, introduces large amounts of steam together with very low heat. The steam-heat atmosphere is gradually altered until the last stage where there is very little steam but high heat. Kiln-dried material is usually reserved for cabinets and furniture and other inside applications. However, the garden woodworker should consider

Softwood grading

including special names for grades of redwood

Examples of domestic softwoods: western white pine, redwood, Engelmann spruce, Sitka spruce, western larch, ponderosa pine, shortleaf pine, sugar pine, white fir, bald cypress, incense cedar, western red cedar.

Classification	Grade	Description
Select	A	practically flawless—excellent choice for stains and natural finishes
	B	similar to "A" but may contain a limited number of small defects—usable for stains and natural finishes
	C	defects that can be concealed with paint are permitted
	D	also usable for paint finishes but will contain more defects than "C"
Common	#1	a good utility lumber that may contain some blemishes and tight knots—standards say it should be free of warp, checks, splits, and decay
	#2	fairly sound wood but may have checks, loose knots and discoloration—no splits or warpage
	#3	medium quality construction lumber—all types of defects are permitted—some bad sections may have to be cut out
	#4	low quality construction lumber—may contain numerous defects of all types—open knot holes permitted
	#5	lowest quality wood used mostly as a filler—considerable amounts of waste often encountered
***Structural**	Construction	the highest quality structural material
	Standard	similar in quality to "construction" but with slight defects permitted
	Utility	poor structural qualities—often used where additional members contribute more strength
	Economy	lowest quality structural material
Redwood	Clear all heart	top quality—one face completely free of defects—opposite face may have no more than two pin knots regardless of board size—excellent stability—usually kiln dried
	Clear	high quality finish lumber similar to *Clear—all heart* but may contain sapwood, some small knots, and medium surface checks—usually kiln dried
	Select heart	all sound heartwood—available in surfaced or unsurfaced condition—usually not kiln dried—knots permitted
	** Construction heart	an economical all-purpose grade—good choice for posts, decks and smaller garden projects—usually not kiln dried
	Select	very similar to *Select heart* but used where termites and decay are not problems
	** Construction common	a good all-purpose material but for above-grade constructions—contains sapwood—knots permitted
	** Merchantable	contains larger and looser knots and more imperfections than other grades—heartwood and sapwood are included in this grade, so some pieces are good for ground-contact projects

Structural lumber is graded mainly for strength
** Often designated as *Garden* grades

it for benches, tables, and similar outdoor projects. Post-construction protective treatments to maintain original quality are wise but we will discuss these later.

Air drying, which is done outdoors with the lumber stacked in special ways to permit free air circulation around each piece, reduces moisture content to about 12% to 20%. Air-dried lumber is quite suitable for general construction work.

Shrinkage

Wood shrinks or swells, gains or loses weight, in relation to its moisture content. In use, where it is exposed to daily and seasonal humidity variations, it is constantly undergoing some change to achieve a balance with the humidity of its surroundings. The purpose of correct seasoning, handling, and storing of wood is to minimize moisture-content variations. Ideally the moisture content of lumber being used should correspond to the average atmospheric conditions to which it will be exposed when the project is completed. A step in this direction is to store your stock according to how it will be used. Keep kiln-dried wood indoors. It's okay to keep air-dried lumber outdoors, but under a cover. In either case, if storage time is lengthy, separate the boards with wooden spacers.

Typical shrinkage, and possible distortion, of various shapes cut from a log are shown in the sketch below. Tangential shrinkage, which occurs in the direction of the annual growth rings, is the most obvious. Radial shrinkage, across the rings, is less, and longitudinal shrinkage, along the grain, is minimal. For example, the dimensions of a board, after drying, would be reduced mostly in width, not so much in thickness, and hardly

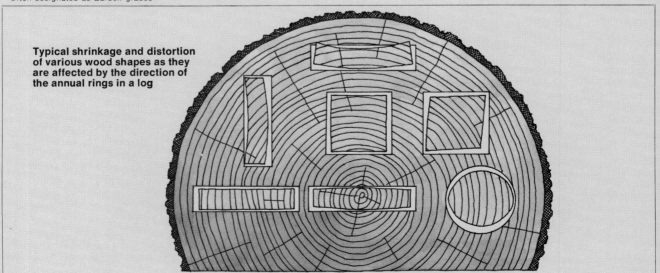

Typical shrinkage and distortion of various wood shapes as they are affected by the direction of the annual rings in a log

at all in length. The sketch further shows how radial and tangential shrinkage combined affects the shape of the pieces.

Shopping

Know the lumber dealer's language and you will avoid confusion and stand a better chance of getting what you want. Softwoods are usually available in standard thicknesses and widths in lengths starting at 8 feet and going to 20 feet in 2-foot increments. The width of 1-inch stock increases in 1-inch increments up to 6 inches and in 2-inch increments from there to 12 inches. 2-inch stock widths increase in 1-inch increments up to 4 inches and in 2-inch increments thereafter.

Thickness and width are always called out in *nominal* dimensions: the size of the board when first sawed at the mill. The *actual* size, what you get, is the same board but reduced by the amount of material removed during surfacing. Thus, a 1x2 will actually measure ¾x1½ inches; a 2x12, 1½x11¼ inches. Generally, the thickness of 1-inch stock is reduced by ¼ inch; 2-inch stock by ½ inch. Widths in both thicknesses are reduced by ½ inch in boards up to 6 inches and by ¾ inch thereafter.

These facts are important when ordering material. For example, two pieces of 2x12 will not provide a slab 2 inches thick by 24 inches wide, but one 1½ inches thick by 22½ inches wide. The only way to get what you actually ask for is to buy lumber in the rough. Here, a 2x4 will truely be 2 inches x 4 inches and often a bit more. Rough lumber is not a bad material for containers, walls for raised beds, headers, and so on. The texture blends nicely with greenery and, depending on grade, kind, and seasoning, lumber in the rough may be cheaper than surfaced products.

The foot . . . board and linear

Many retail lumberyards now place a price tag on each piece of wood, yet the cost is always figured, and quoted, on a board foot basis. A board foot is simply a piece of wood that measures 1x12x12 inches. If the thickness is 2 inches, then the piece contains two board feet. To find the board feet in any piece of wood, multiply the nominal thickness in inches by the nominal width in inches by the actual length in feet and then divide by 12. Thus a 2x4-inch x 16 foot piece at 36 cents a board foot contains 10.67 board feet and costs $3.84.

Use the same formula to compute price per board foot if the quote is on a linear foot basis. Twenty feet of 1x6

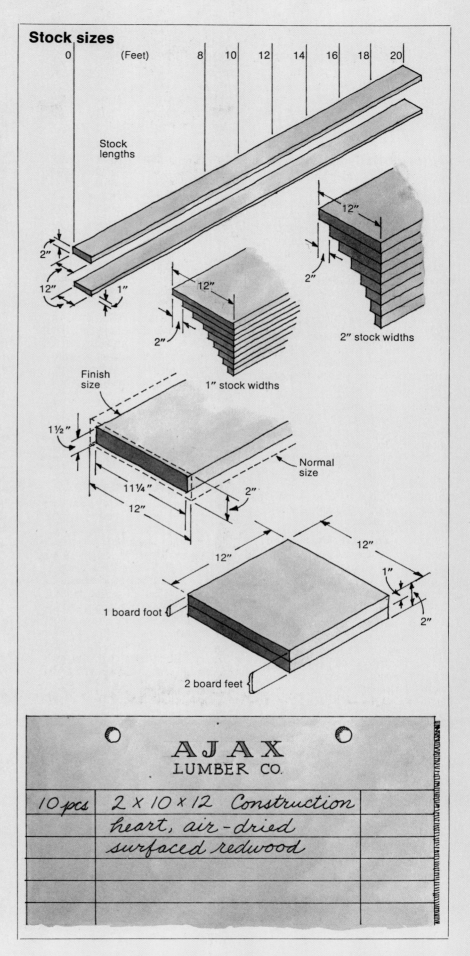

Stock sizes

Stock lengths

1″ stock widths

2″ stock widths

Finish size

Normal size

1 board foot

2 board feet

AJAX LUMBER CO.

| 10 pcs | 2 x 10 x 12 Construction heart, air-dried surfaced redwood | |

at 30 cents a linear foot costs $6. The board contains 10 board feet—$6 divided by 10 equals 60 cents a board foot.

If you are buying large quantities, the price quoted may be so much per thousand. The "thousand" refers to board feet.

Professionally speaking

To describe the size of the material you want, state nominal thickness by nominal width by actual length, and in that order. Be specific about kinds of wood, grade, seasoning, and finish. Your order should read something like: 10 pieces of 2x10x12 construction heart, air-dried, surfaced redwood. If you talk the language you won't be misunderstood and if you are, your complaint will be justified.

For the types of projects this book is about, it's best to order by the piece instead of by board or total linear footage unless you wish to establish an inventory for future building; a sort of private lumberyard.

Don't order pieces that must be cut to a nonstandard length. If you need a number of 5-foot pieces, order 10-foot stock and do the cutting-to-length yourself. You'll be charged extra if the lumberyard must do it for you. If you need a 6½-foot piece, order the standard length that comes closest to it. You can use the remainder on some other project.

Buy and use wood carefully. The scrap pile of the true lover of wood doesn't contain much more than kindling.

Typical exceptions to the above buying considerations are dowel, lath, and molding. Dowel is purchased by diameter in standard lengths, usually 3 feet. Lath is supplied by bundles containing so many pieces, so many feet long. Molding is always sold by the linear foot.

On using plywood

Plywood is a practical garden-project material and is available in as many grades and kinds as lumber. Large panel sizes, usually 4x8 feet, make it especially useful for fabricating project components that are wider than the normal, maximum 12-inch width of lumber. Often, it can be cheaper to use than a similar amount of solid material. Usually thicknesses range from ¼ inch to ¾ inch but it is available in thinner or thicker panels. It's also possible to get panels longer than 8 feet; even special sizes like a 5x9-foot sheet, which is just right for table tennis.

There are several construction considerations which apply specifically to plywood used outdoors.

✓ All material must be EXTERIOR grade. The veneers in such panels are bonded with waterproof glue and are back-stamped with the word "exterior."

✓ All plywood edges should be sealed. This can be done with a suitable commercial water repellent and decay retardant, or with a paint product, or even with a coat of waterproof glue.

✓ Many types of plywood house-siding panels are attractive and usable for garden projects but some are factory treated with water repellents and decay retardants which contain chemicals, like pentachlorophenol, which are toxic to plants. How long the toxicity remains is a variable, so when using such materials for containers and the like, it's wise to line the interiors with polyethylene film or to coat them with liquid asphaltum or a material like pruning paint.

It's wise to take such precautions regardless of the material involved because they afford a protective barrier between soil and wood.

Utilizing readymades

By "readymades" we refer to those specialty items which can be purchased and used, as is, as project components or add-ons that dress up an otherwise plain assembly. The bins and racks of lumber dealers and home-supply centers contain many varieties of legs, turned posts and spindles, carved trim strips and plaques, even filigree and die-cut panels with matching, grooved framing members. It will pay for you to browse through such sections to become familiar with what is available.

You can often find pieces that would be impossible for you to make without an advanced woodworking tool. A fiddle back or three-leg stool with turned legs requires a lathe if the job is done from scratch. The project is more feasible if all you have to do is shape the top and then add legs that are already turned.

Embossed or carved trim or even simple molding can transform a basic, butt-jointed container into a more decorative, more professional-looking project.

The idea is to let the readymades spark your imagination. Don't view them as bits and pieces in a bin but as design details and structural elements.

Garden joints

If we emphasize only a few joint designs it's because they do the job and are relatively easy to make with minimum tools and time. Actually, any joint the craftsperson chooses, from a butt to the classic dovetail, may be used in garden projects.

A factor in joint selection is the amount of glue area it affords. A miter is often used at corners but it is chosen more for appearance than strength; it doesn't have much more glue area than a butt. In both cases there are methods of reinforcement (see sketches on page 84) to use should the project require it.

Parts that cross, X-shaped leg assemblies for benches or tables, for example, can be joined surface-to-surface or they can be made stronger by using one of the lap joints shown on page 83. The latter take more time but the shape of the joint itself adds an antitwist factor. The U-shaped cut can be made in one piece, or in both if you prefer that the crossing surfaces be flush.

The dado is made just like the lap except that it is usually longer and narrower—sized to fit the insert piece. It's a good joint to use for pieces like shelves since it provides more glue area than a butt joint and a ledge for the horizontal member to rest on. The usual substitute for the dado in this type of situation is a wooden cleat for shelf support.

The rabbet is always used at corners. It provides more glue area than a butt joint and serves to conceal most of the end grain of the piece it is attached to. That is one reason why it is often used on plywood constructions.

Nails, screws, irons, and the like, are good joint reinforcements but you should not overlook the advantages of the dowel. It often provides the locking and anti-separation advantages of more complex designs like the mortise-tenon and dovetail, yet it can be accomplished with basic tools. To avoid the accuracy requirements of drilling separate holes that must meet on assembly, hold the parts together and drill through both at the same time.

Example: to dowel-reinforce parts that cross. Hold the two pieces together and drill through. Two holes are better than one since they eliminate the pivot action of a single dowel. Separate the parts so you can clean away wood chips; coat mating surfaces and the dowels with glue; reassemble the pieces. Always use dowels that are a bit longer than necessary;

How to do special joints

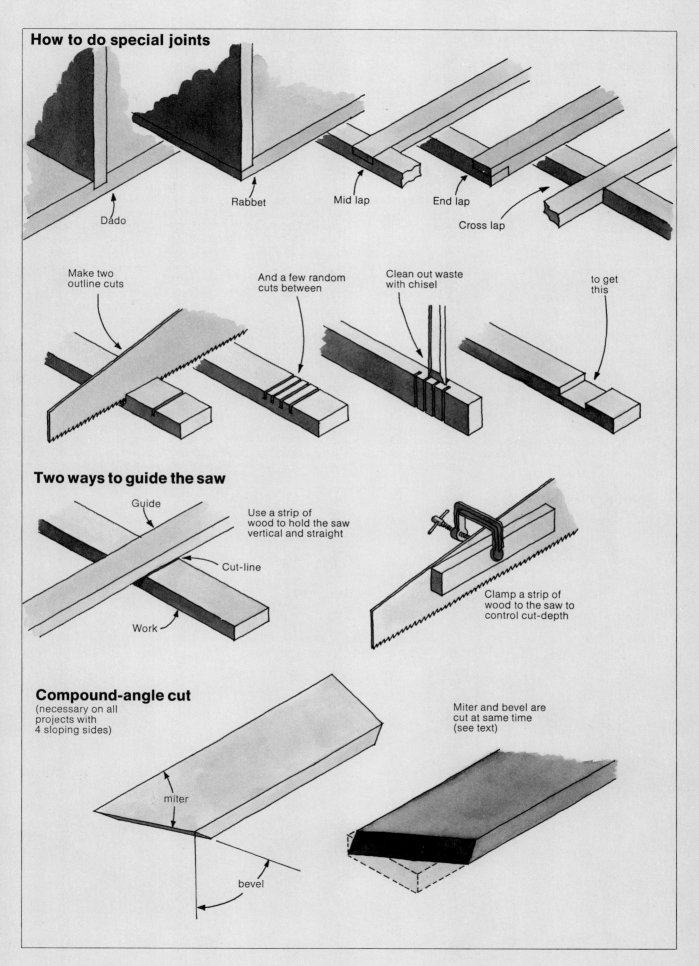

Dado

Rabbet

Mid lap

End lap

Cross lap

Make two outline cuts

And a few random cuts between

Clean out waste with chisel

to get this

Two ways to guide the saw

Guide

Use a strip of wood to hold the saw vertical and straight

Cut-line

Work

Clamp a strip of wood to the saw to control cut-depth

Compound-angle cut
(necessary on all projects with 4 sloping sides)

Miter and bevel are cut at same time (see text)

miter

bevel

you can sand them flush after the glue dries or you can leave slight projections to serve as design details.

The choice of dowel diameter when pieces are joined surface-to-surface is fairly arbitrary but if you are drilling into an edge, the dowel diameter should not be more than ⅓ to ½ the thickness of the part.

The corners of containers, or any box with sloping sides, require compound angle cuts if they are to fit properly, regardless of whether you use butt or miter joints. This may be difficult to visualize but will be apparent at assembly time if you ignore the rule.

The compound angle is a combination of bevel and miter, the degrees-relationship changing as the slope-angle of the project changes. Example: you are working with a portable electric saw and are building a butt-jointed container with sides that slope 20 degrees. Tilt the saw blade to 6¼ degrees and mark across the stock for a miter of 71¼ degrees. Saw across the line as you would for any crosscut and the result will be a compound angle that is just right for the project. If a miter joint is involved, use the same miter setting but change the tilt to 41¾ degrees.

For a second example we'll assume a container with sides that slope 30 degrees. For butt joints, use a blade tilt of 14½ degrees and do a miter of 63½ degrees. If the joint is mitered, stay with the same miter angle but change the blade tilt to 37¾ degrees.

Remember that the above examples are for 4-sided containers. Both the blade-tilt angle and the miter change as you increase the number of sides in the project.

The secret of good joinery, simple or complex, is for the parts to mesh without being forced. Even a butt joint won't look right or do its job if you try to use nails or screws, glue or clamps to compensate for poor cuts.

The glue to use

Of the many types available, those of most interest to the garden woodworker should be either *water-resistant* or *waterproof*. Why choose? Why not waterproof all the way? It's simply that waterproof glues are usually more expensive than other types and the extra cost may not be justified. If you are building a picnic table for use on a porch or under a solid overhang, then water-resistant glue is okay. If the table is intended

for permanent exposure on a patio, then waterproof glue makes sense.

The following are capsule descriptions of readily available wood glues, including some which have no water-resistant virtues. After all, as a woodworker you may be inclined to make some projects for indoor use.

The familiar white glue, widely available in plastic squeeze bottles, is a polyvinyl resin that is always ready to use. It sets up rapidly at room temperature and is colorless so it leaves an invisible glue line. It has good strength but is not water-resistant and tends to soften at high temperatures.

The old hide glue has lost much ground since the introduction of synthetics but is still used by professional cabinetmakers and plays a part even in some commercial furniture industries. It is available in liquid form in plastic squeeze bottles. It is not waterproof but it has enough body to act as a gap filler. Its strength is very good and it's slow setting so you have plenty of time to put parts together.

Casein glue, from milk curd, is a tan powder you mix with water. It has good strength and can be applied at any temperature above freezing. It is highly water-resistant, though not waterproof. It is often chosen as the

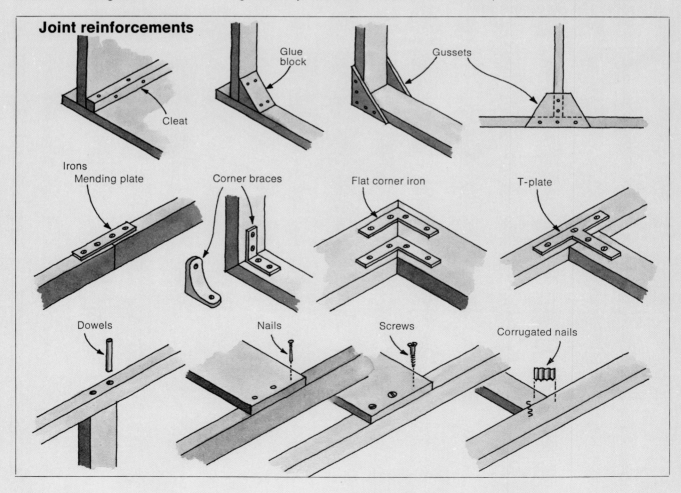

Joint reinforcements

Glue block

Gussets

Cleat

Irons
Mending plate

Corner braces

Flat corner iron

T-plate

Dowels

Nails

Screws

Corrugated nails

adhesive for oily woods but it should be used with care on woods like redwood, oak, and maple because it can stain those species.

Plastic resin glues are ureaformaldehyde adhesives that come in powdered form and are mixed with water for use. They contribute much strength in joints and are very water-resistant. The glue is nonstaining and will set in about four hours.

Resorcinol resin glue is completely waterproof and comes as a two-component product, one being liquid resin, the other a powdered catalyst. The two combined result in an extremely strong adhesive widely used for outdoor projects, boats, and general structures exposed to water and extremes in temperature.

Epoxy resins are also two-part resin-catalyst products. They are waterproof and provide strong adhesive qualities—fine for joining wood to wood, and for joining wood to masonry, ceramics, metal, and plastics.

Application of glue

Always read the instructions on the label of the container. We must assume the manufacturer knows how his product will perform in optimum fashion. If the label tells of an ideal temperature application range, then you take a chance if you choose to work at below or above the extremes.

Be sure all mating surfaces are coated uniformly. It's okay to squeeze glue from a bottle in a wavy line or a series of beads, but then spread it properly with a sliver of wood or a small brush. A double application may be in order at the end of a board because it absorbs more glue than the edges or surfaces. A certain amount of glue squeeze-out is normal when joint parts are put together but an excess is wasteful. Any glue that escapes from the joint should be removed immediately with a sharp knife or chisel, and any still remaining should be cleaned off with a cloth dampened with warm water. Glue left where it should not be will behave as a sealer, preventing even penetration of stains or other finishes.

Nails

Until the day comes when wonder adhesives replace mechanical fasteners, nails will continue to be popular wood connectors. This is because of proven performance and the extensive variety in size, shape, finish, and material to suit any application. The garden woodworker's interests are served by materials or finishes that hold up outdoors without rusting or staining. Included are materials like aluminum alloy and stainless steel; the most common, adequate finish is hot-dipped galvanizing. There are others, but do remember: generally, the key word for fasteners used outdoors is "noncorrosive."

The chart below describes most commonly used nails. Not shown are *box* nails, which are similar to *common,* but have smaller heads and thinner shanks. Box nails are good to use when the heavier common nail causes the wood to split. Common and box nails, because of their broader heads, have more holding power than *finishing* or *casing* nails. Confine the use of the latter to projects where you wish to set the nail below the surface of the wood so you can conceal it with some form of wood filler. Threaded nails come in all types and sizes and are designed to provide more holding power than plain-shank varieties. *Cut* nails are more expensive and not as available as others, but they can add interesting touches to projects if you use them judiciously.

Nails

Size	Length	Gauge			App. # Per Pound		
		Common	Finishing	Casing	Common	Finishing	Casing
2d	1"	15			850		
3d	1¼"	14	15½		540	880	
4d	1½"	12½	15	14	290	630	490
5d	1¾"				250		
6d	2"	11½	13	12½	160	290	245
7d	2¼"				150		
8d	2½"	10¼	12½	11½	100	195	145
9d	2¾"				90		
10d	3"	9	11½	10½	65	125	95
12d	3¼"				60		
16d	3½"	8		10	45		70
20d	4"	6			30		

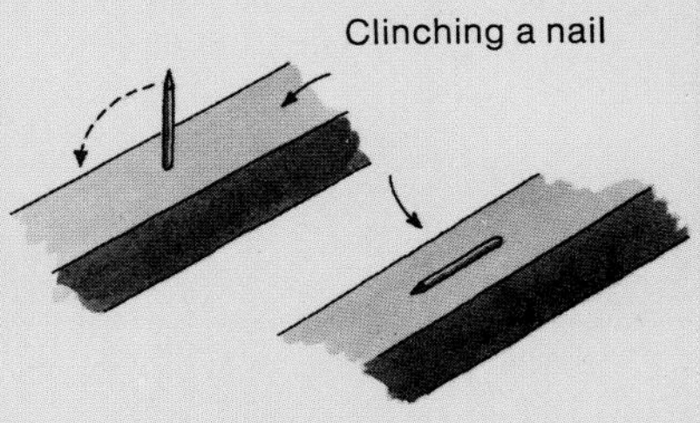

Clinching a nail

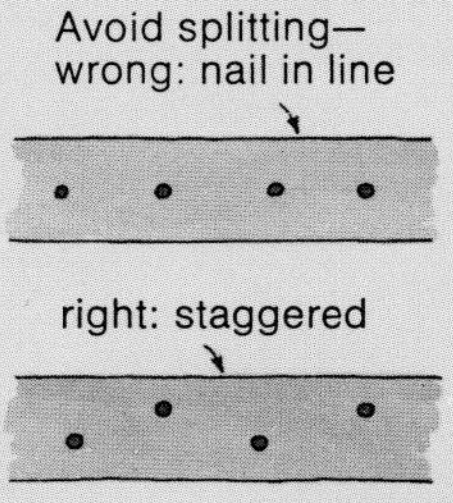

Avoid splitting—
wrong: nail in line

right: staggered

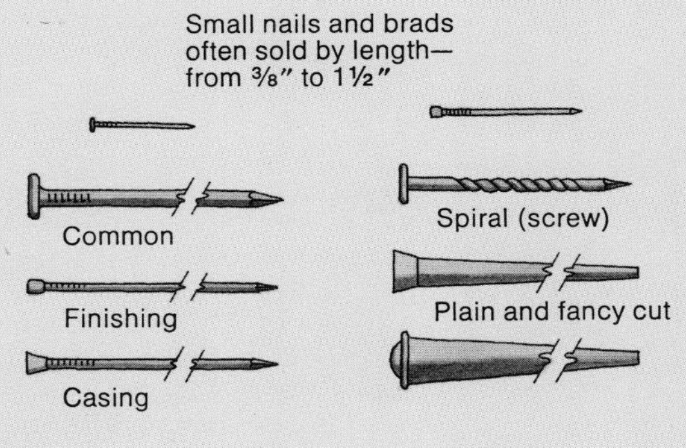

Small nails and brads often sold by length— from ⅜" to 1½"

Common

Finishing

Casing

Spiral (screw)

Plain and fancy cut

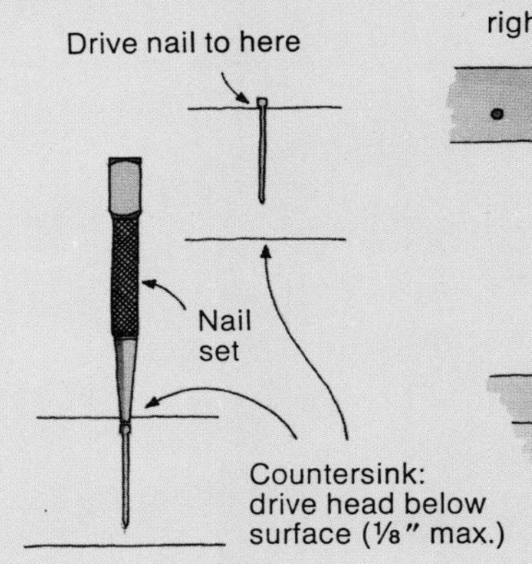

Drive nail to here

Nail set

Countersink: drive head below surface (⅛" max.)

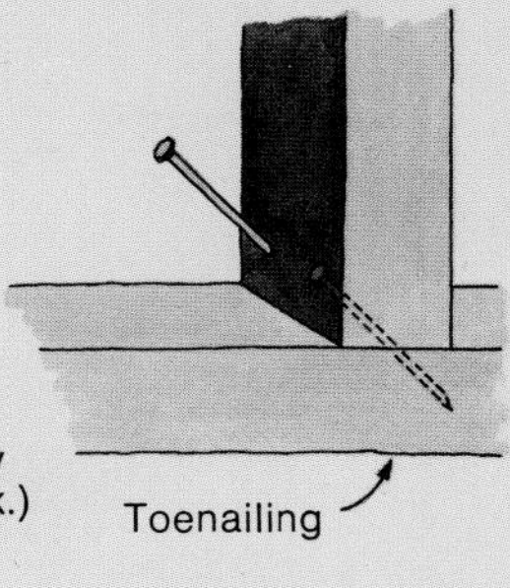

Toenailing

Screws for softwood

Screw Size		Lengths Available	Drill Required For Shank Hole		Drill Required For Pilot Hole		Best Screwdriver For Tip Width
#	Dec. equiv.		#	frac.	#	frac.	
4	.112	¼"-1½"	32	7/64	55	3/64	⅛"
5	.125	⅜"-1½"	30	1/8	53	1/16	3/16"
6	.138	⅜"-2½"	27	9/64	52	1/16	3/16"
7	.151	⅜"-2½"	22	5/32	51	1/16	3/16"
8	.164	⅜"-3"	18	11/64	48	5/64	¼"
9	.177	½"-3"	14	3/16	45	5/64	¼"
10	.190	½"-3½"	10	3/16	43	3/32	5/16"
12	.216	⅝"-4"	2	7/32	38	7/64	⅜"
14	.242	¾"-5"	—	¼	32	7/64	⅜"

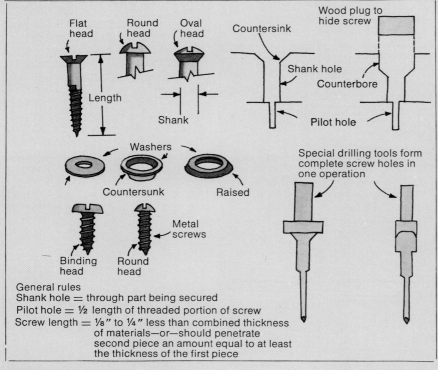

Flat head · Round head · Oval head

Length · Shank

Countersink · Wood plug to hide screw · Shank hole · Counterbore · Pilot hole

Washers · Countersunk · Raised

Special drilling tools form complete screw holes in one operation

Metal screws · Binding head · Round head

General rules
Shank hole = through part being secured
Pilot hole = ½ length of threaded portion of screw
Screw length = ⅛" to ¼" less than combined thickness of materials—or—should penetrate second piece an amount equal to at least the thickness of the first piece

Bolts

Type	Diameters Available	Lengths Available	Where To Use Washers
MACHINE BOLT	¼" to over 1"	½" to over 10"	under head and nut
STOVE BOLTS flat head or round head	⅛" to ½"	⅜" to 6"	under head and nut with round head; under nut with flat head
CARRIAGE BOLTS	3/16" to ¾"	½" to over 10"	under nut
LAG BOLTS (or screws)	¼" to 1"	1" to over 10"	under head

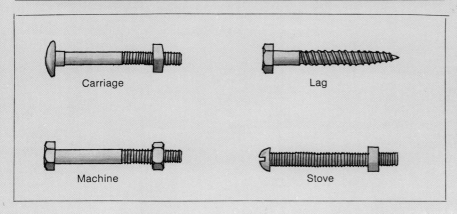

Carriage · Lag · Machine · Stove

The general rule for choosing a nail length: it should be three times as long as the thickness of the part being fastened. It's a good rule but not always practical. For example, to follow the rule you would have to use 4½-inch nails when joining 1½-inch stock surface-to-surface. This would allow 1½-inch of the nail to project. Here, and in other similar situations, some judgement is called for. In the above situation, use a 10d or 9d nail. You'll find that the length of nail called for by the rule becomes more startling as the thickness of the wood increases, so be wise when making a choice. Break the rule when the assembly requires it.

Don't try to show how fast you can drive a nail. More, and lighter, blows are better than a few strong ones. Stop hitting headed nails as soon as they are flush with the wood. Those few extra-insurance blows some of us love to deliver do nothing but damage the wood. Stop driving finishing and casing nails *before* the head is flush; finish the job with a nail set, sinking the head a maximum of ⅛ inch.

Some wood splits easily but so can all types, especially when nailing is done close to an edge. Old timers tried to prevent splitting by tapping the point of the nail with a hammer to blunt it slightly, but even this doesn't always work. The best solution, if the situation demands it, is to drill small holes before you drive the nails. Avoid driving nails on a common centerline, especially when they are in line with the grain of the wood. A staggered nailing pattern is less likely to cause splitting. Don't continue to drive bent nails; remove them and straighten them, or use new ones.

Nails that are longer than the total thickness of the parts can be clinched on the back when appearance is not a factor. This just means that you bend and then hammer flush the part of the nail that projects. The practice should not be frowned on since it adds a considerable amount of strength to an assembly. Often, it solves a nailing problem. For example, a ½-inch brad will not hold crossing, ¼-inch-lath strips together for long. A 1-inch nail, clinched on the back, will provide long-lived security.

Screws

Screws hold better than nails but require more time and special techniques for correct installation. Tapping a screw with a hammer to start it is very poor practice. Maximum strength and minimum driving problems result when you start the job by drilling the shank and pilot holes listed in the chart on page 86. These call-outs are very specific but not so critical for our projects that you can't fudge a bit. When you don't have exactly the right size drill, choose the one that comes closest—preferably on the minus side. Follow as closely as possible the general rules outlined in the chart.

Flathead and oval head screws call for a beveled indent which is accomplished with a countersink—a special tool you can use in a hand or electric drill. It's customary with softwoods to stop the countersinking a bit short of the actual screw-head size. Driving the screw will sink it far enough to make up the difference. The procedure assures that the screw will be flush with, not below, the surface of the wood.

Screws are often concealed with wooden plugs, or short lengths of standard dowel, but the technique calls for counterboring to form a seat for the plug. A good procedure to follow is this: drill the pilot hole through both pieces and then enlarge the hole in the top piece to shank-hole size. Using the shank hole as a center, work with a twist drill or a spade bit to enlarge the shank hole to ½ inch in diameter and to a depth of ¼ to ½ inch. Coat the counter-bored area with glue after you have driven the screw and tap home a piece of dowel which is a bit longer

than the depth of the hole. Sand the dowel flush after the glue dries, or round off its edges and allow it to project as a design detail. You can change the above procedure if you find it more convenient. Do the counterbore first, then the pilot hole, and then the shank hole. Each tool used will provide a center point for the next drilling operation.

Special tools ("Screwmates") are available so you can do the whole job in one operation. They come in various sizes so you can choose one to suit the screws you are working with.

Washers are used to increase the holding power of the screw. Use flat washers with round head screws; countersunk types—flush or raised—with flat head or oval head designs.

Bolts

Bolts are heavy-duty connectors. They pull and hold parts together more strongly than either screws or nails. They can be unfastened easily and are good for projects you may wish to disassemble. All the types shown in the chart on page 86 are suitable for garden projects if they are made of, or coated with, a noncorrosive material.

The two most useful ones are the *carriage* and the *lag*. The oval head on the carriage bolt is more decorative than a square or hex head. The shoulder under the head, which sinks into

and grips the wood, makes it possible for the bolt to be tightened or removed with a singe wrench. Base length selection on the total thickness of the parts being joined, plus about ½ inch for a washer and nut. Drill holes that match the bolt's diameter.

View lag bolts as oversize, super-gripping screws. While they are often used as wood-to-wood connectors, they are especially useful when a project must be attached to a house wall, fence, or masonry. In the latter situation, expansion shields, forced into holes in the masonry, are used in combination with the lags.

Pilot holes are required whenever you use lag bolts in wood. The hole size depends on the density of the wood and also on how close to an edge you are working, but it is seldom less than 50% of the bolt's diameter. Best bet, whenever you are in doubt, is to run a test with scrap pieces of wood.

Miscellaneous hardware

There are more types than those shown on page 84 and the art below. The items selected for the chart are on the basis of their application to projects in the book. The corner braces and irons are joint-reinforcement items. When you buy, select only those (and screws) which are noncorrosive.

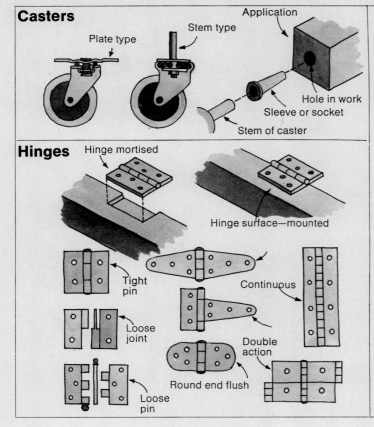

Casters

Plate type — Stem type — Application

Hole in work — Sleeve or socket — Stem of caster

Hinges

Hinge mortised — Hinge surface—mounted

Tight pin — Continuous — Loose joint — Double action — Round end flush — Loose pin

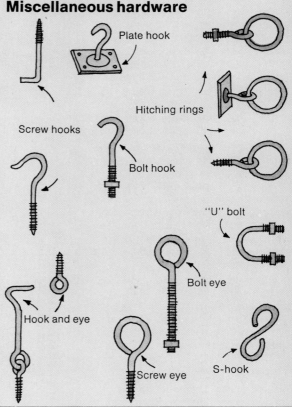

Miscellaneous hardware

Plate hook — Hitching rings — Screw hooks — Bolt hook — "U" bolt — Bolt eye — Hook and eye — Screw eye — S-hook

The hook and eye is a simple solution to keep a door or a lid closed but it will work efficiently only if the hook and the eye are in correct alignment and if the eye is positioned so the hook requires a little force to become seated.

Screw eyes and hooks, and bolt eyes and hooks, do similar jobs. The difference is that the former are turned into wood as if they were wood screws while the others are passed through holes and secured with nuts.

S-hooks are functional as connectors for lengths of chain, or may be used with hitching rings for hanging containers.

U-bolts serve to hold round items like pipe or dowel to other materials. The legs pass through holes you drill; tightening the nuts forces the U-bolt tightly against the item being secured. Pipe clamps, shown in use on the COMPOST BIN (page 74), work in similar fashion but are fastened with regular screws.

All of the items are available in different sizes so you're sure to find one to suit the project on hand.

Hinges

All the hinges shown are available in materials or with coatings that are non-corrosive, and may be surface-mounted or set flush in mortises. There is great variety of sizes so choosing one for a particular project is never a problem.

When choosing a butt hinge, decide if you may want to remove the panel or door at some time. A loose joint or loose pin version will let you do that without having to remove screws. *Don't* use them if security is a factor.

The strap hinge, T-hinge, and round end hinge are often substituted for the butt on outdoor projects because they supply a decorative, rustic detail.

Continuous hinges—often called piano hinges—are available in lengths up to 7-feet. They distribute stress more evenly than separate hinges and so contribute a safety factor on long doors or lids that are used frequently. The storage version saw horse on page 48 is an example of where a continuous hinge might be better than butt hinges.

The double action hinge, used on the trellis on page 32, lets adjacent panels of a project fold against each other like an accordion pleat. It's wise to use three of these along an edge instead of the usual two.

Casters

Casters, under containers for example, do two things—they serve as legs

Tools

Tool	Basic functions	Closest power tool equivalent	
		Portable	Stationary
*CROSSCUT SAW 26" x 10 pts.	cutting across the grain of the wood—also for miter cuts & plywood	cut-off saw equipped with combination blade	table saw—radial arm saw
RIP SAW 26" x 5½ pts.	cutting with the grain of the wood		
*COMPASS SAW 12" or 14"	cutting curves—doing inside cuts	saber saw	jigsaw band saw
DEEP FRAME COPING SAW	doing curves more intricate than you can accomplish with the compass saw		
*CLAW HAMMER 16 oz.	driving and removing nails		
NAIL SETS 1/16" and ⅛"	driving nails below wood surfaces so they may be hidden with wood dough		
*FLEXIBLE TAPE 8' minimum	measuring materials—marking dimension points		
*COMBINATION SQUARE	marking cut-lines—checking assemblies		
*BRACE w/¼", ⅜", ½", ¾", 1" bits	boring holes for bolts, dowels	*⅜" drill w/variable speed & reverse switch—	drill press
HAND DRILL w/points from 1/16" to about 3/16"	drilling small holes—holes for screws	set of spade bits	
*SET OF SCREW-DRIVERS	driving and removing screws	above drill w/set of screwdriver bits	
WOOD BUTT CHISELS— ¼", ½", 1"	joint work—some shaping		
SCRATCH AWL	marking dimension points—location of screw-holes—starting holes for small screws		
*SET OF OPEN-END WRENCHES OR AN ADJUSTABLE WRENCH	tightening nuts when using bolts		
BENCH PLANE—10"	smoothing edges—doing chamfers and bevels	plane	jointer
HALF ROUND BASTARD RASP W/HANDLE—10"	rounding off edges—shaping—roughing for distressed look	rotary rasp attachment for drill	
HEAVY-DUTY HAMMER W/RIPPING CLAW— 20 or 22 oz.	driving large nails, spikes, small stakes—separating nailed boards		
SLEDGE HAMMER— 8 lbs. w/30" or 32" handle	driving large stakes		

Those marked * are first-choice items

Hand tools

Crosscut saw

Combination square

Brace and bit

Rip saw

Hand drill and point

Compass saw

Screwdriver

Screwdriver bit

Deep-frame coping saw

Wood chisel

Nail set

½ round bastard rasp

Claw hammer

Measuring tape

Scratch awl

Hammer w/ripping claw

Sledge hammer

Adjustable & open end wrenches

Bench plane

Power tools

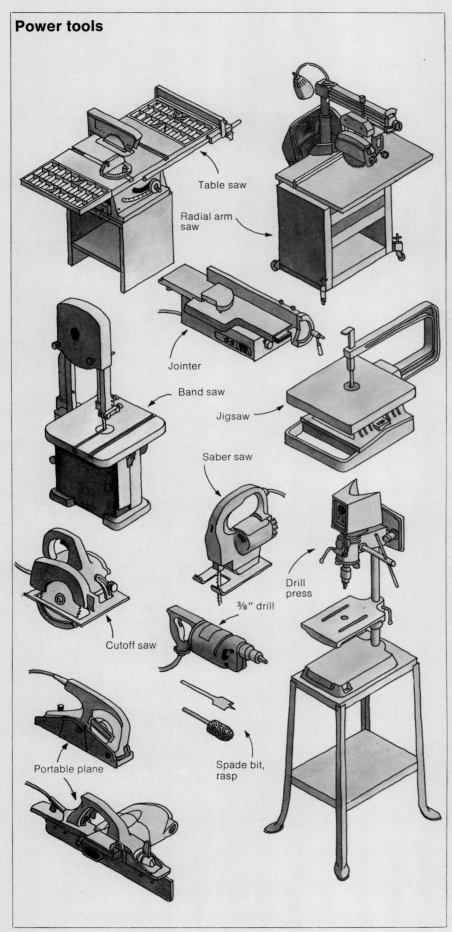

Table saw

Radial arm saw

Jointer

Band saw

Jigsaw

Saber saw

Cutoff saw

3/8" drill

Drill press

Spade bit, rasp

Portable plane

to raise the project above grade and they make the project mobile. Stem varieties cost less than plate types but should be considered mostly for light-duty applications. Wheel diameters vary; generally, the larger wheels support more weight. In either case, look for two features— a swivel action so the wheel can turn in any direction, and wheels made of hard rubber or iron. Plastic wheels are okay on slick surfaces but wear quickly on textured concrete.

Plate types are attached with screws—stem types lock in sleeves driven in holes formed in the work. The size of the hole equals the outside diameter of the sleeve. Drill the hole deep enough to take the full length of the stem.

Tools...more or less

You can build any of the projects in this book if you own a hammer and a saw and have something, like a thumb, to measure with. However, plans (not necessarily just those in *this* book) would have to be changed to suit tool limitations. With just a hammer, you could use only nails. With just a plain saw, you could cut only straight lines. You would need an old tar's knowledge of knots to make the swing on page 73 without drilling holes—plus a lot of energy and saw-skill to form notches and such without the use of a chisel.

Yet, the jobs could be done, so reasons for owning a nice set of tools go beyond the ingenuity of doing with a few. There are such factors as more convenience, less production time, and easier-to-achieve-accuracy. It's important that garden woodworking be fun, which it won't be if you try to drive screws with a kitchen knife or bore holes with a swizzle stick.

Our list of hand tools on page 88 isn't extravagant in numbers or cost even if you do the professional thing and buy top-quality products.

If you are involved in woodworking, you already have tools and supportive arguments for your choices. If you are just beginning, we have a few suggestions. Those tools marked with an asterisk (*) are basic and necessary. In the hole-drilling area you can choose between the brace and the portable electric drill. The latter is high on the list because you can use it with spade bits, twist drills, and hole saws to form any size hole up to about 2½ inches. With accessories, it's also useful for other chores, like sanding, wire brushing, rasping, even paint mixing and sawing.

Other power tools are listed for information only. Chances are that if

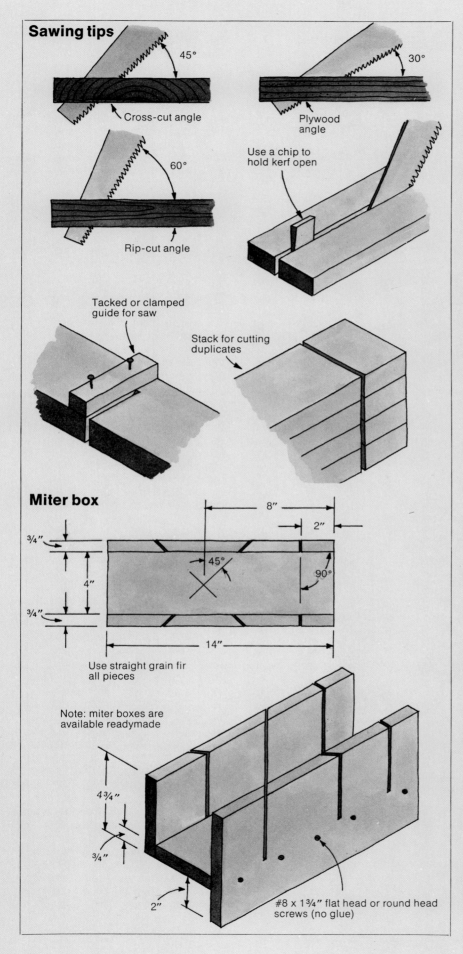

Sawing tips

45°
Cross-cut angle

30°
Plywood angle

60°
Rip-cut angle

Use a chip to hold kerf open

Tacked or clamped guide for saw

Stack for cutting duplicates

Miter box

8"
2"
¾"
4"
¾"
45°
90°
14"

Use straight grain fir all pieces

Note: miter boxes are available readymade

4¾"
¾"
2"

#8 x 1¾" flat head or round head screws (no glue)

you become totally involved in woodworking you will acquire power tools as well as hand tools. The first buy for garden woodworkers is usually a portable electric saw, convenient to use outside as well as inside.

Always buy quality tools. You will gain in the long run because a cared-for, good tool will last indefinitely and will be more pleasant to work with.

Saw good . . . like you should

Most woodworking problems are caused right off by bad saw cuts, the principal contributing factor being a desire to rush the job. Saw-teeth, rip or crosscut, are engineered to remove just so much wood and won't do more no matter how you force the blade. Forcing results in jammed teeth, buckling blades, and inaccuracies of cut. Correct sawing technique calls for reasonable, steady strokes. Support the work firmly and take a comfortable stance that permits free and easy strokes. Hold the cut-off piece as you near the end of the cut to avoid splintering, which will occur if you allow the piece to fall free.

You get smoothest crosscuts if you work so the blade-to-wood angle is about 45 degrees. A more acute angle is better if you are sawing plywood; there will be less tearing of surface fibers. A 60-degree angle is better when you use a rip saw. There will be a tendency on long cuts for the kerf (groove formed by the blade) to close. Keep this from happening and binding the blade by using a chip of wood, or even a large nail, to hold the kerf open.

Cuts will be more accurate, if you use strips of wood as saw guides. These can be any straight pieces of 1- or 2-inch stock, clamped or tack-nailed to the work so an edge is on the cut-line. The guide lets you cut straight and helps you keep the saw vertical. When possible, stack pieces to do duplicate cuts. For example, to square the ends or to get two similar lengths of 1-inch stock, hold the boards together and cut through both at the same time.

Keep saw blades clean and smooth. Our trick is to polish them frequently with paste wax. This prevents rust and reduces friction. Take saws to a professional for resharpening as soon as you feel they are dulling. Working with dull tools is very poor practice and isn't safe.

The miter box

The miter box, detailed in panel is one of the most useful sawing accessories. It is designed mainly for accurate cutting of molding but may be used with any flat stock or dowel that fits in it. With ours we can cut stock up to 4 inches wide. You can make the base wider if you like, or make a second version so you can handle bigger pieces.

The accessory is usually used with a backsaw but will be as efficient if made for a crosscut saw. Just be sure the saw used to cut the guide grooves is the one that will be used with the jig. Construction accuracy is critical. If the grooves are not cut correctly, work sawed in the box will not be accurate. Lay out the cut-lines by using a combination square. Mark the lines across edges *and* down the sides so you'll have a guide through the entire cut. If you are wondering why the drawing says "no glue" it's so you can replace a damaged part of the box if it becomes necessary.

Drilling hints

Like sawing, drilling should never be forced beyond the cutting capacity of the bit being used. Bits for a hand brace have screw points and pull themselves into the wood almost automatically. Do not use bits with screw points in a power drill. Work with twist drills or spade bits and use only enough feed pressure to keep the tool cutting. Drill speeds should decrease as the size of the hole increases. Spade bits are an exception. They work best at high speeds (between 1000 and 2000 rpms) regardless of size.

Always back up your work with a scrap piece of wood. This will minimize, if not prevent totally, the splintering that occurs when the bit breaks through. When possible, drill holes through duplicate pieces by stacking them. Keep your hand holding the work well out of the path of the bit.

The outdoor work bench

Your outdoor workbench should be as portable as the tools you use and this pretty much calls for a pair of sturdy sawhorses. Two make sense since they can be used to support long boards and may be spanned with a sheet of plywood to serve as a work table.

Our section on SAWHORSES tells you what you should know about constructing them and also illustrates some unique nonworkshop uses. 24 inches is a good height when the horse is strictly for sawing. This permits a stance that places you over the work so you have a good view of the cut-line, and can stroke freely.

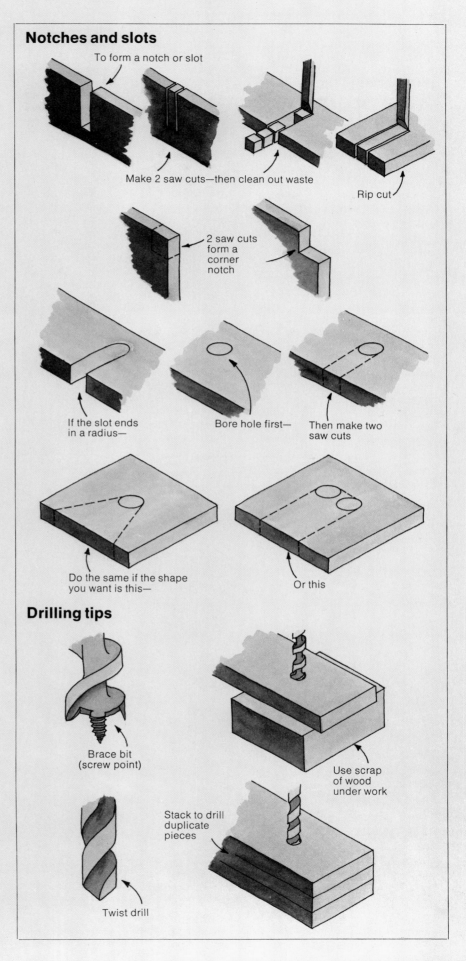

Notches and slots

To form a notch or slot

Make 2 saw cuts—then clean out waste

Rip cut

2 saw cuts form a corner notch

If the slot ends in a radius—

Bore hole first—

Then make two saw cuts

Do the same if the shape you want is this—

Or this

Drilling tips

Brace bit (screw point)

Use scrap of wood under work

Stack to drill duplicate pieces

Twist drill

If you make the horses about 28 inches high, they can be used as supports for table tops. The increase in height will not eliminate them from use as sawing supports.

Wood protection and finishing

There are three basic considerations
✓ Will there be soil-contact or alternate cycles of wet and dry conditions? If so, choose a wood that is naturally resistant to decay and insect attack, or supply a barrier.

✓ Do you wish to preserve the natural appearance of the wood? Here, a transparent finish is the way to go.

✓ Do you wish to change the appearance of the wood by adding color, or texture, or age? Here, you think of exterior-type paints, antiquing techniques, creative doings that add a special visual appeal.

The heartwood of cedar, cypress, and redwood may be used, as is, in soil-contact situations. Other woods, even though some may have moderate resistance to decay, should be treated with a preservative. The preservative may be applied by brush, but generously and preferably with applications repeated until the wood will absorb no more. This is especialy important when the wood, or a part of it, will actually be buried.

Be aware that preservatives containing copper sulfate will impart a green tone to the wood. This is not objectionable in burial situations or on the inside surfaces of containers, but you may not like it elsewhere. Others may contain pentachlorophenol, which is toxic to plants for a variable period of time. When these are used, allow at least two weeks between application and planting. All such materials should be used strictly in accordance with the instructions on the label. Toxic agents can be harmful to humans as well as greenery.

Other preservation methods include painting inside walls with a tar substance, or lining them with sheet plastic. These ideas make sense because you can get to the planting quickly—as soon as the plastic is in place or the tar substance is dry. A plastic liner is especially useful when a container wall is more than one board high. The liner keeps water from leaking through the joint.

When the weather provides a finish

Any unprotected wood will undergo a color, texture and, usually, physical change when exposed to the weather. Among the bad things that can happen when only one side of the board is fully exposed, are cupping (a warp across the width) and a tendency to tear loose from fastenings, especially nails. Among the good things are a pleasant change in color, usually on the grayish side, and the appearance of a patinalike sheen.

Surface erosion, which may be viewed as a natural texturing, takes place very slowly. Many, many years may pass before a board loses a measurable amount of thickness. The degree of, and the pattern of texturing, will vary with different kinds of woods, as will the extent of color change. There can be differences in boards cut from the same tree.

Cedar generally takes on a light gray color and a silvery sheen. Redwood can go through several color changes depending on climate. In a damp or humid atmosphere, it may first darken but eventually bleach to a driftwood gray. If the project is completely sheltered from rain, the wood may stay dark for its lifetime. Unfinished redwood will gradually turn a silvery tan when the climate is consistently dry.

Ponderosa and western white pine become light gray and acquire a moderate sheen. White fir and Douglas fir become dark gray but acquire little sheen. Checks caused by weathering are more conspicuous on western larch, eastern and western white pines, ponderosa pine, than they are on cedar, bald cypress and redwood. Redwood ,Douglas fir, white fir, cypress, and cedar are examples of woods that cup less than others.

If you don't want the wood to weather for a while, apply a water seal to all pieces of wood, even before assembly. This assures that concealed areas will be as protected as exposed ones. If you prefer to allow some weathering, at least treat concealed areas right at the start—especially on projects such as containers.

Water seals rank high among clear finishes for outdoor projects. They are easy to apply and do as much as any product to maintain the original appearance of the wood. Many of them contain a mildew-resistant element and this is good since mildew can cause discoloration on any material.

Wood protection

Painting with preservative

Coat inside with tar

Plastic liner

Heavy, high-gloss finishes don't seem at home outdoors. If you have a yen for a varnish-type product, we suggest you dilute it heavily with the correct solvent and make several light applications instead of a single, thick one.

This also applies to linseed oil. Full-strength applications will probably not be totally absorbed by the wood. A tacky, even gummy residue may remain on surfaces.

Bleaching treatments are often listed in natural-finish categories. These are ready-to-use commercial products that react chemically with the wood to produce a driftwood-gray appearance. This is generally the result although effects vary from one wood to another. The results are most apparent when the wood is dark to begin with. Bleached finishes often last forever. Redoing is necessary only if the wood darkens.

Coloring

Pigmented stains are a popular garden-woodworking finish because they permit a controllable color change without concealing the true nature of the wood. In essence, they bridge the gap between a natural finish and a paint job. Color control is obtained by choosing either a light-bodied penetrating stain or a heavy-bodied variety that has hiding power akin to paint. In each case, application methods are a factor. You can dilute the stain with the correct solvent. You can apply it heavily by brush and allow it to dry, or wipe it off with a cloth after a few minutes so you get a color tone without hiding the wood grain. The elapsed time affects the darkness of the color. You can also apply the stain with a cloth. This allows more control than working with a brush.

Water seals may be used under or over a stain, depending on the product. The seals that can be applied first often require a considerable drying period before the stain can be added. As always, it is very important to read instructions on labels before using the products.

Some people like a paint finish on outdoor projects, some don't. The principal objections are that paint hides the wood and the coating must be renewed periodically. If you decide on paint, select one specifically designed for exterior use. You have a choice of oil base or water emulsion varieties in matte or glossy finishes. Avoid heavy applications because a thick coat has a tendency to crack

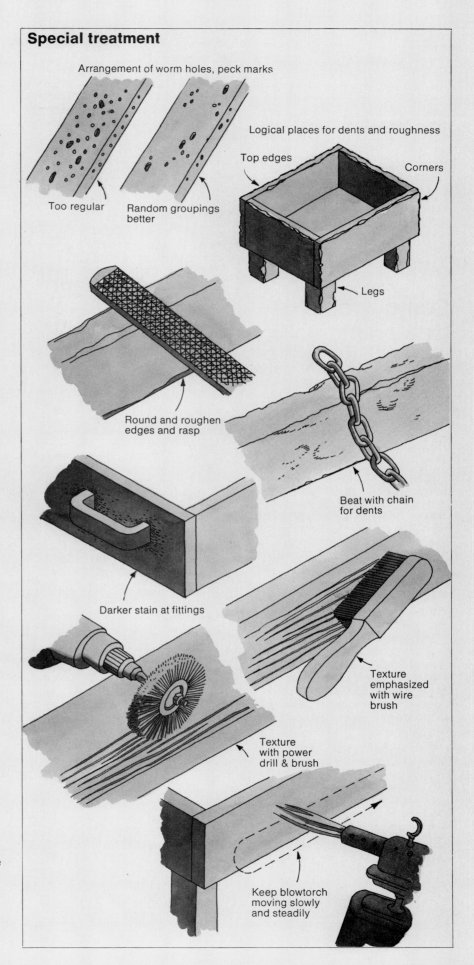

Special treatment

Arrangement of worm holes, peck marks

Too regular

Random groupings better

Logical places for dents and roughness

Top edges

Corners

Legs

Round and roughen edges and rasp

Beat with chain for dents

Darker stain at fittings

Texture emphasized with wire brush

Texture with power drill & brush

Keep blowtorch moving slowly and steadily

and peel. How many initial coats you apply depends on the covering power of the paint and the kind of wood, but it's usually wise to apply a prime coat first. This is often called out as an "undercoater" and it may be tinted to match the color of the final coat. If you choose to paint redwood, always use an oil or alkyd base primer no matter what type of finish paint will be used.

Be sure that wood surfaces are dry before you apply paint. Never do a paint job in the sun. Don't expose the project to the sun's rays until the coating is dry. If you must paint a fixed project outdoors, time the chore so the sun's rays do not strike the painted surfaces during or immediately after painting.

Some special treatments

The person who takes the off-beat trail may see and do exclusive things, but he may also fall off a cliff. When you move away from the norms you should temper adventurousness with a degree of caution. If you are ever in doubt about a particular treatment you dream up, try it out first on a scrap piece of wood.

Walnut stain looks pretty good on pine but you should not try to hide the fact that the wood *is* pine. Use the stain for color toning, not for concealment. A cluster of tiny holes drilled in selected areas to resemble worm holes is okay, but perforating the entire project would be an overstatement.

Use-worn wood usually has rounded edges and a dent or two. You can create these effects on new boards by working carefully with sandpaper, or a file or rasp, and by whacking the wood in several places with a short length of small chain, but don't overdo it. First judge where these use-indications would occur normally and confine the effects to those areas.

Projects may have normal-looking darker areas near handles and often around pieces of hardware and fasteners. To imitate this when staining, just apply a heavier application in those areas but be sure to blend in so the tone change is not startling.

If there is a particular color tone you want and can't find it in a stain, select a paint that does the job but dilute it drastically with the correct solvent and use it as you would a stain. This way, you can tint wood from pure white to deep black without hiding the grain.

You can texture any wood so it looks like it has been abraded by wind and sand simply by working it over with a wire brush. This is easiest to do with a rotary brush chucked in a portable drill and is particularly effective on woods having hard- and soft-grain areas, like fir. The soft grain removes easily and the three-dimensional result is quite attractive. Rotary brushes are available with either hard or soft bristles so control of the texturing is possible through choice of tools as well as how hard you bear down when you work.

A burned finish is attractive, and easy to do if you work with a propane torch. Here again, it must not be overdone. Keep the torch moving steadily and far enough away from the wood so the flame just chars. Work so results are darkest around corners and near joints. You can preview results if you practice the technique on scrap pieces. Go over the project with sandpaper or steel wool before you apply a finish.

Working safely

Take your time when doing anything and never forget that tools, wood, sunshine, and finishes don't think; that's your job. Read all instructions that might come with a tool and obey them; not just at first, but always. It's a fact of woodworking that you can be in more danger as you become more proficient. It's okay to be confident, but not if it makes you careless.

It makes sense to buy portable electric tools that are double-insulated. Extension cords should be heavy-duty and have a grounded connection. Wear safety goggles whenever there's a chance of flying particles. Don't wear loose clothing, work barefooted, or go hatless if the sun bothers you. Be sure you have adequate ventilation when using any finishing material. Seal all containers immediately after use. Use only those solvents that are recommended on the label.

We're often more relaxed with hand tools than with power tools. It's true the latter can do damage more quickly, maybe more extensively, but it's not the degree of harm we should be concerned with but the fact that accidents should not happen at all. A handsaw, a screwdriver, a hammer, will function no matter what is placed in front of it. Probably the greatest safety factor of all is visualizing what will happen if you have a finger where wood alone should be.

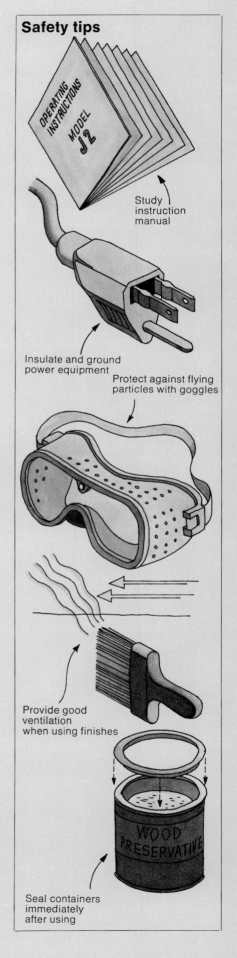

Safety tips

Study instruction manual

Insulate and ground power equipment

Protect against flying particles with goggles

Provide good ventilation when using finishes

Seal containers immediately after using

Woodworker's illustrated glossary

Woodworkers, like gardeners, have special words and names that relate to various activities. Some terms are common in all areas, others have limited application. This is not a glossary for a house builder or an inside-furniture maker, but for our gardener-woodworkers. Many items and operations have been illustrated throughout the book, especially in the shop section. Here are others—some repeated for emphasis—some we mentioned but did not show.

Check

Cup warp

Center line

Edge distance

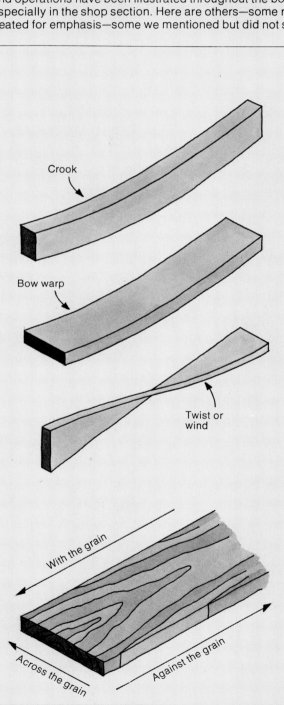

Crook

Bow warp

Twist or wind

With the grain

Across the grain

Against the grain

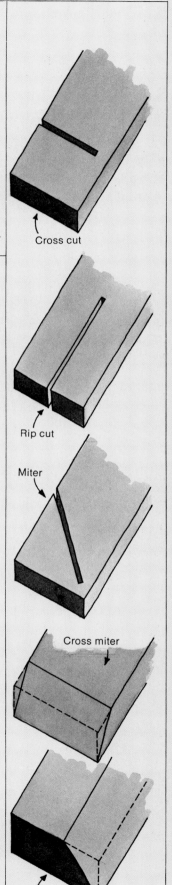

Cross cut

Rip cut

Miter

Cross miter

Bevel

Illustrated glossary

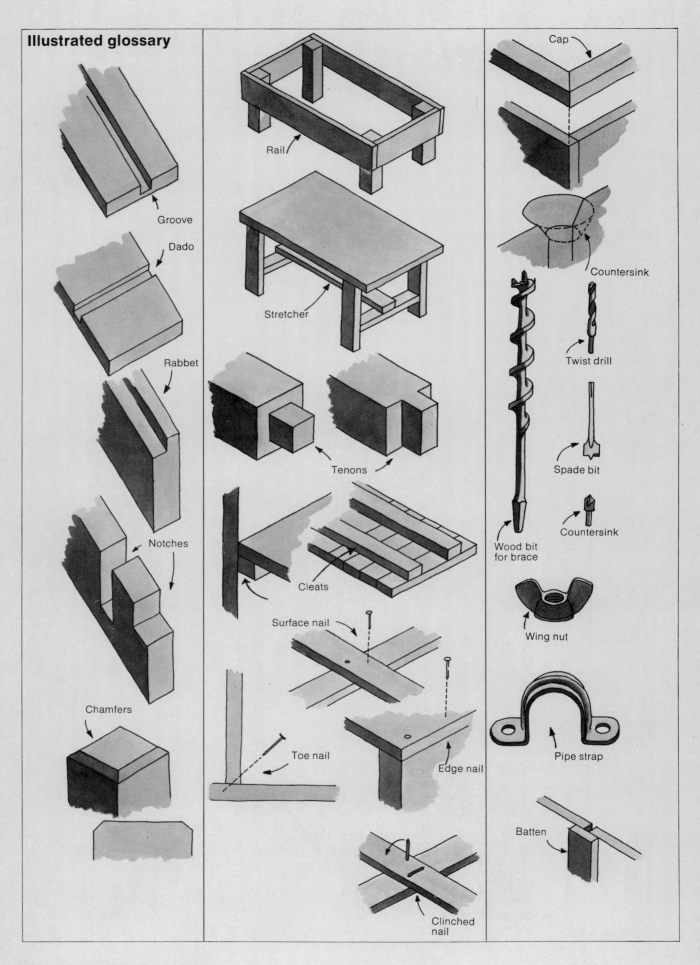

Groove

Dado

Rabbet

Notches

Chamfers

Rail

Stretcher

Tenons

Cleats

Surface nail

Toe nail

Edge nail

Clinched nail

Cap

Countersink

Twist drill

Spade bit

Countersink

Wood bit for brace

Wing nut

Pipe strap

Batten